95 -

LEXINGTON BOOKS - REVIEW COPY

HEATH

A Raytheon Company

QUAN.	CATALOG NUMBER	TITLE	PUB. DATE	LOCATION	PRICE
1	004489-X	CRIST FUTURE AMERICAN ENERGY POL			18.95

JUN 21 2 46 PM '82

NO CHARGE - REVIEW COPY

IF THIS BOOK WAS SENT FOR YOUR REVIEW, PLEASE SEND 2 COPIES OF YOUR

REVIEW TO: LEXINGTON BOOKS - REVIEW EDITOR

D.C. HEATH AND COMPANY

125 SPRING STREET

LEXINGTON, MASSACHUSETTS 02173

PLEASE FOLD OVER ON FOLD MARKS AND FASTEN AT BOTTOM, SO RETURN ADDRESS ON BACK IS OUR

BUSINESS REPLY MAIL

FIRST CLASS   PERMIT NO. 6332   LEXINGTON, MASS.

POSTAGE WILL BE PAID BY ADDRESSEE

D. C. HEATH AND COMPANY

LEXINGTON BOOK DIVISION
125 SPRING STREET
LEXINGTON, MA 02173

☐ We plan to review this book.
Issue (if possible) _____

☐ We would like to receive your general catalog.

☐ We would like to receive notices in _____ category.

☐ Please correct address as follows:

_____

_____

_____

PLEASE LET US KNOW THAT YOU RECEIVED THIS COPY BY
RETURNING THIS REPLY CARD. ALSO PLEASE NOTE IF YOU
REQUIRE FURTHER INFORMATION OR ASSISTANCE.

HEATH

PLANNERS LIBRARY
ASPO
1313 E 60TH ST
CHICAGO IL

60637

COMMENTS:

Future American
Energy Policy

Future American Energy Policy

Edited by
Meredith S. Crist
Arthur B. Laffer
University of Southern California

LexingtonBooks
D.C. Heath and Company
Lexington, Massachusetts
Toronto

Library of Congress Cataloging in Publication Data

Main entry under title:
    Future American energy policy.

    1. Energy policy—United States—Congresses.   I. Crist, Meredith S.
II. Laffer, Arthur B.
HD9502.U52F87   333.79′0973′   80-8992
ISBN 0-669-04489-x   AACR2

Copyright © 1982 by D.C. Heath and Company

Published simultaneously in Canada

Printed in the United States of America

International Standard Book Number: 0-669-04489-x

Library of Congress Catalog Card Number: 80-8992

Contents

Preface and Acknowledgments

Future American Energy Policy derives from a program of opinion and analysis entitled "Energy Future: Policies and Consequences," presented 21-22 February 1980 at the University of Southern California, Los Angeles, under the joint auspices of the university's Center for the Study of Private Enterprise and the Atlantic Richfield Company.

The objectives of the Center for the Study of Private Enterprise are to develop a continuing program of research and information about America's private enterprise system and the role of incentives in a market economy. The center, formed in 1976, is dedicated to the belief that free political and economic systems are crucial to the continued stability and growth of America's economy and essential for the well-being of its citizens.

Since the private enterprise system is an integral part of our free society, dissemination of economic education is a key function of the center. The Center for the Study of Private Enterprise has increased its scope to include public policy research. In this capacity it has approached a reasoned and thorough study, through knowledgeable presentations and discussion, of the world energy situation.

The Atlantic Richfield Company engages principally in the exploration, production, and transportation of crude oil and natural gas, and the refining, marketing, and transportation of petroleum and petrochemical products. Headquartered in Los Angeles, Atlantic Richfield is recognized as one of the nation's foremost corporations taking innovative interest in the social and cultural activities of both the California community and the country as a whole, and it has concerned itself with the problems and challenges of the economic and regulatory processes that face the world of the future.

As the world faces a deeply troubling energy shortage, nations and individuals alike have articulated meaningful and penetrating questions with regard to local, state, and national policy on energy matters. What have been the social and economic costs of past energy policy? What have we learned? What paths should business, government, and industry follow? What kinds of cooperation and coordination are needed to best implement these decisions and unknown coming events?

To answer these questions with depth and insight the Energy Future conference brought together some of the nation's most perceptive and experienced people from business, public life, and public advocacy groups. They probed the intricacies of one of the most complex problem areas to challenge our life-styles—and imaginations—in many decades.

Participants in the program did not need to confirm the existence of America's energy problems—although there is considerable difference of opinion as to its causes and effects—and proceeded directly with observations, proposals, and possible solutions. Because of its complexity and the degree to which energy supply permeates our social, cultural, and economic fabric, invited speakers were selected from a wide spectrum of American society.

The editors wish to acknowledge their thanks to the University of Southern California for providing its facilities, and to the Center for the Study of Private Enterprise and Atlantic Richfield Company for their expertise in arranging for the interaction of energy-conscious people from business, government, and academia.

Introduction

As any analyst or news reporter in the energy field is aware, energy conferences have proliferated over the last seven years. Certain speakers' names appear on slick invitations with predictable regularity. The topics of these symposia are so familiar that many seasoned conference-goers can recite the substance without attending the session.

No conference can adequately cover all energy-related topics and still attract time-conscious participants and audiences. The result is a conference structure that develops from the sponsor's special interest. Topics tend to be fuel-source oriented (with solar conferences held separately and not interacting with geothermal or synfuel meetings), or action-oriented (like conservation workshops), or technique seminars, such as for modeling or other academic interests.

Future American Energy Policy offers a refreshing and unique departure from these types of conference proceedings. It is based on an energy symposium that dared to combine groups that rarely interact at a public forum. The participants included public-opinion commentators, leaders from civic and social-conscience groups, congressmen, and researchers, as well as domestic oil executives, foreign oil producers, and government regulators.

Using a format of five primary presentations, each followed by a panel commentary and debate with audience questioning, the interaction at the conference brought about a rich diversity of information and views. We believe that no other single book presents so much insight in so concentrated a form.

The book starts with Dr. Meredith Crist, an energy economist at the University of Southern California (USC), who provides an overview for the subsequent articles. She aptly integrates the global and domestic energy situation from the perspective of options facing the United States. In chapter 2, Congressman David Stockman, now director of the Office of Management and Budget, condemns economics professors for the damaging energy myths they have been perpetuating. His remarks contain a wealth of information on the effects of misguided energy policies and a rousing exhortation to reexamine our basic assumptions, particularly on foreign-oil dependency.

In part II, chapters 3 to 5 are essays on the social implications of energy policy. Moderator Eddie Williams, of the Joint Center for Political Studies, Washington, D.C., points out that while economic and political aspects of energy policy receive the lion's share of attention, social impacts are more wide reaching. John Naisbitt, of the social-opinion research firm Yankelovich, Skelly and White, and now head of the Naisbitt Group, comments on societal restructuring. He explains several "overarching macro trends," including regionalism/nationalism, centralization/decentralization, and the impact of ours becoming an information society.

In chapter 4 the NAACP's Margaret Bush Wilson interweaves her concern regarding immediate problems of minority Americans with the imperative need to promote global cooperation between developed and developing countries. Hers is a searching plea for keeping international development and trade motives at the forefront of our energy-policy deliberations.

In chapter 5, L. Calvin Moore, of the Oil, Chemical and Atomic Workers International Union, delivers a forceful review of the failure of oil-company management and government to keep energy prices in line with real costs. His is an indictment of the energy shortages of 1973 to 1974 and 1979 and an analysis of inequalities occurring in the consumer utilization of energy.

In part III the economic implications of U.S. energy policy are addressed. Jude Wanniski, well known as a conservative business consultant, in chapter 6 presents a cogent case for instituting more control over U.S. monetary policy and encouraging international trade—after an exhaustive expose of America's austerity rhetoric, international monetary excesses, and progressive taxation. Chapter 7 contains the views of Atlantic Richfield's Dr. David Sternlight, who expounds the deleterious effects of recent energy policy. He calls the windfall profits tax a revenue-generating excise tax that will become all too necessary for future federal budget needs. His analysis shows that federal energy policy has neither stimulated supply sources nor discouraged energy-demand growth. In chapter 8, Andrew Safir, then director of California's Office of Economic Policy and now in private business, discusses regulatory goals and procedures, comparing Japan's environmental economic approach with that of the United States. He argues persuasively for allocation mechanisms in times of crisis. The controversy generated by these panelists culminates in heated debate with Congressman Stockman.

Part IV begins with international attitudes. Moderator Abdul-Rahman of ARCO Petroleum Products asks key questions still unresolved in the U.S.-international energy forum. The First Under Secretary of Egypt's Ministry of Petroleum, Dr. Hussein Abdallah, comments that oil-producing countries must adopt a longer time horizon for their decisions than oil consumers (chapter 9). He eloquently traces the history of grievances of the OPEC nations and succinctly analyzes the progress of dialogues and cooperation between oil-exporting and oil-consuming countries. Dr. El Mallakh, of the University of Colorado's International Research Center for Energy and Economic Development, in chapter 10 thoughtfully outlines the problems of low absorptive capacity characteristic of many oil-exporting nations. He concludes that countries ranging from Iran to Mexico to Norway will set oil-production levels and revenue receipts consistent with reasonable internal development objectives. The Iranian revolution of 1979 following too rapid inflow of revenues and pressures on a society unreceptive to modernization serves notice of the dangers of too much wealth too quickly.

In chapter 11, Eric Zausner recounts his experiences as head of the Federal Energy Administration under President Ford. Now with the international management consulting firm of Booz, Allen and Hamilton, he itemizes the lessons the United States should have learned. His remarks are a humorous indictment of federal energy policy and planning horizons.

Part V features an optimistic "least-cost" energy strategy. In chapter 12, Roger Sant, director of Carnegie-Mellon's Energy Productivity Center, shares his personal delight and sense of encouragement from studies conducted by his organization. He stresses that opportunities abound, and the United States is only beginning to experience conservation under private initiatives, efficiency in appliances and buildings, and appropriate shifts in resource use and institutional improvements. Moderator Edward Myers, of the Southern California Edison Company, points out that institutions have to change, but electric utilities have been steadfast in providing uninterrupted service for almost a century; he is then challenged to moderate among three feisty contributors.

Dr. Walter Mead (chapter 13), an economist and professor of economics, brashly accuses many of simply mouthing conservation, missing the precise meaning of the term. In defining conservation as appropriate use of resources over time so as to maximize their net present value, he supports the existing price mechanism. Chapter 14 contains the well-formulated and concentrated thinking of Laurence Moss, consultant on energy and environment policy, former Sierra Club president, and now participant in the National Coal Policy Project. Moss argues that energy producers and environmentalists can achieve their goals by meeting on common ground. He is optimistic about decentralization as a solution to energy problems so they may be ameliorated by pertinent local factors. Congressman Timothy Wirth in chapter 15 reminds Americans they can take pride in the country's environmental progress. He urges that large energy projects—such as synfuel and coal development in his home state of Colorado—use private and public partnerships to minimize the adverse impacts inherent in the creation of complete industries and acceptable living communities where none existed before.

By the way of furnishing concluding remarks in part VI, Dr. Arthur Laffer, professor at USC and originator of the Laffer tax-reform curve, gives a dynamic account of how American presidential economic policies run counter to the public's perception, and rewrites the Robin Hood legend to demonstrate the role of economic disincentives (chapter 16). Dr. Laffer concludes that past neglect of the economy's supply-side for demand-side management has made us all poorer. In chapter 17, Thornton Bradshaw, former president of Atlantic Richfield and now of RCA, somberly comments that the oil industry has been regulated ("crippled") for so long he has to support gradual decontrol, subsidized synfuels, and an energy mobilization board. He is optimistic, nevertheless, on achieving a future balance of environmental concerns with increased production.

The editors are pleased to present such rich diversity of expertise and debate. We feel the benefits of such interaction should lead to a more balanced approach in future energy policy.

Part I
Challenges

1 A View of the Problem

Meredith S. Crist

Hundreds of speeches, articles, and books have touted the energy crisis as the focal topic of the 1970s, following Viet Nam in the 1960s and the Cold War in the 1950s. Energy-related developments, raising oil prices fifteen-fold, have had a dramatic impact on economies, international relations, and the social fabric of many countries. These economic, international, and social issues are addressed by the collection of articles in this book. This introductory chapter sets the stage for the book's collection by characterizing the history of future energy scenarios, summarizing their current status, and assessing the likelihood of a return to normalcy with an energy future requiring little guidance. (Energy analysts customarily hypothesize exogenous policy and political events over a specified period which result in a set of energy prices revolving around some reference energy source, usually Middle East oil FOB the Persian Gulf [net of transportation costs]). Given these exogenously determined prices and events, they try to determine both how the demand for energy will grow and what supplies will be forthcoming.)

The future outlook for energy and attendant economic, international, and social implications has been universally viewed with concern throughout the last decade, with the concerns heightened depending on the specifications implicit in the viewer's mind. Widely divergent domestic manifestations of these concerns can be seen in policies such as depletion allowance elimination, pricing and entitlements regulations, the strategic petroleum reserve, windfall profits tax, threatened allocative programs and antitrust actions, mandated thermostat settings and other standards, and a host of public conservation education programs.

Such a wide array of policies derived from the increasing divergence of experts' opinions over the last decade with each advance in conservation practices and each price shock in the world oil market. A review of a sampling of various and sundry predictions from many sources for the 1990s onward reveals that the extremes of the energy crisis are no longer in vogue and one-by-one are being retracted, ignored, or scaled down in a return to normalcy: "We're running out of oil and the internal combustion engine is doomed—no one will be driving a car as we know it today. . . ." "We will all live, work, and entertain ourselves in single multipurpose, ecologically-balanced buildings. . . ." "There will be windmills atop all skyscrapers and solar photovoltaics on every roof. . . ." "The earth will be surrounded by space stations beaming electricity to earth. . . ." "Russia will be consuming more energy than it produces and will take over the Middle East. . . ."

"Gasoline rationing and mandated maximum automobile sizes are inevitable. . . ."

These and other less dramatic views can be characterized in three scenarios comprising many factors, opinions, and policy alignments. While oversimplified, the following scenarios are summaries of historical thought and have ongoing worth in assessing the current outlook: gloom-and-doom will prevail if we do not encourage the energy supply side; renewables and conservations will contribute significantly to our energy future; free markets, if given a chance, will save the day.

Gloom-and-Doom Scenario

This is an alarmist view of shifting supply-and-demand balances, Middle East political volatility disadvantaging the United States, and insignificant domestic impact of renewables or conservation. Specifically, world demand for oil is increasing with far-reaching implications attaching to major shifts in demand-supply balances. The most obvious example is the Soviet Union. Presently exporting 1.5 million barrels per day (mbd) to its Communist neighbors, Russia's oil supply-demand balance is expected to shift. Central Intelligence Agency (CIA) studies have warned that the Communist bloc will become a net oil importer by the mid 1980s.

With the ever-present internal volatility in the Middle East, the potential for interruption of oil supplies to the Western countries becomes a priority issue. Forty percent of non-Communist oil traffic flows through the Straits of Hormuz, with Saudi and Kuwaiti oil blocked should the straits be shut down. The alarmist view includes a further ingredient of either pervasive Soviet movement into the Middle East, or a stalemate between the United States and the USSR in which the United States would be constrained to stay neutral if our Middle East interests were threatened.

On the world supply side major oil discoveries have occurred in the North Sea, Canada, and Mexico. However, the United States cannot expect other countries' internal goals to be subjugated in favor of increased oil production for American benefit. They will not be our saviors and have made that fact apparent.

Alarmists point out that domestic oil production peaked in 1970 at 9.6 million barrels per day (mbd). Since 1970, production has declined 10 percent and would be much greater if Alaskan supplies had not started in 1977. The decline is projected to continue as old fields peak out and as more expensive secondary and tertiary oil recovery methods are required. New fields are more difficult to find, require deeper drilling (for example, offshore), or development in hostile (Arctic) environments.

Further gloom-and-doom prospects accompany each of the other energy sources in addition to the basic oil situation. Progress on each fuel source—oil, gas, nuclear, coal, solar, geothermal, wind, tidal, ocean thermal, synfuels, and practices such as conservation and utility load management—has been below the high expectations of the early 1970s. The pessimistic perceptions of the gloom-and-doom camp can be summarized as follows.

Nuclear power, once viewed as the single major energy contribution to the future, has undergone a public reassessment. Following the 1978 Three Mile Island accident, as well as other safety incidents and increased government regulations, projections of the contribution of nuclear power have been scaled down by a factor of ten from the expectations of the 1960s.

For industries and utilities, coal was nominated in the 1980 *Annual Report to Congress* as the fuel source to offset the reduced contributions from oil, gas, and nuclear energy. Nonetheless, increased coal use faces several obstacles. Mining and transportation safety concerns, environmental pollution, flue-ash disposal, and the issue of carbon-dioxide global greenhouse effects are ingredients in the gloom-and-doom future vision.

Synfuel, shale, and tar sands development also are firmly under gloom-and-doom, the economics of such technologies escalating as fast as the inflation rate. In hindsight, if these facilities had been constructed in the mid 1970s, their output would be economical after several OPEC price hikes in the late 1970s. But if constructed now their costs place their output at marginal profitability given the environmental problems. In fact, out of several hundred bidders for government subsidies under the Synthetic Fuels Corporation, very few would continue development alone.

The alarmist view consistently places a low likelihood on supply contributions from renewable energy sources. Solar energy has encountered technological barriers, and cost targets have not been met. Solar-thermal-electric central station powerplants are not viewed as viable, with demonstration plants proving to be poor economically. Likewise, government-sponsored research on solar-satellite power and ocean-thermal systems has stopped. Solar-photovoltaics production in the private sector has made less progress than anticipated, with the major companies now concentrating on international sales rather than domestic. Solar-thermal panels are being produced, but their contribution has never been expected to be a significant addition to U.S. energy supplies.

Environmental, safety, and cost obstacles are similarly present in implementing wind-energy potential. While many small systems have been installed, large wind-energy systems have technical and safety problems with rotor blade design. Additionally, all wind systems are characterized by intermittent electrical output, visual aesthetic disadvantages, and television signal interference.

Geothermal energy production is progressing but at a slow rate, with most favorable resources located far from electric-load centers.

Finally, the gloom-and-doom view had seen energy conservation as an inferior option, with energy savings either a one-time lump sum or nonpersisting savings forced by nonoptimal government-mandated programs and incentives. Given that private conservation initiatives are now mounting, the alarmists bemoan the delay in decontrol policy and still expect conservation responses to be drawn out slowly over the long run.

In summary of the gloom-and-doom view, the world energy demand and supply forces threaten national security, the U.S. supply side relies on conventional fuel supplies and U.S. oil production is declining, energy conservation potential on the demand side is de-emphasized, and renewable sources will not contribute much. U.S. use of coal and nuclear power are offered as saviors despite growing environmental and safety problems. This is a grim view of this country's ability to survive oil-supply disruptions in the coming decades, much less to achieve energy independence.

Scenario of Multiple Energy Options

This scenario asserts the likelihood of significant contributions in this century from a diversified portfolio of options for both the demand and supply sides. Such options include a multitude of technologies in three general categories of conservation, renewable sources, and synthetic fuels. The controversial aspect of this scenario is not the likelihood of a diversified outcome, but the timing and weights of each option. Of the three categories, only conservation is clearly a winning option.

Conservation

Perhaps more than any other topic, conservation has increasingly dominated the discussions of the energy crisis. While arguments raged over whether its definition should encompass price-induced behavior and what public mandates on private behavior would be tolerated, the energy consumption growth trends have slowed dramatically as a result of private initiatives. Each year forecasts of energy usage are revised downward as historically estimated price elasticities of demand have underestimated the cumulative conservation and price effects of rising energy prices. Thus the contribution of conservation (including price effects) is demonstrably large.

The proponents of this scenario stress a continuing large potential with conservation investments providing cheaper savings in Btu's (British thermal units) per dollar of investment compared to developing new energy sources. (For example, cogeneration options alone are referred to as the "Alaska of the lower 48.")

Renewables and Synthetic Fuels

This second scenario has stressed the need for and large contribution of solar (including wind and hydro) energy up to 20 percent of U.S. consumption by the year 2000. But progress on renewable technologies and synfuel development has not been as rapid as most proponents of this scenario expected. Most private manufacturers are directing their investments to foreign markets. Thus, although the general diversification characteristic of this scenario will undoubtedly come true, the timing and weighting of the components are unlike most proponents' claims. Nonetheless, the view that renewables and synfuels will be a keystone continues to be held widely.

Free-Market Scenario

The theme of this scenario has been that an energy crisis exists only if prices are not allowed to seek levels where markets clear or energy demanded equals energy supplies. This scenario asserts that if prices were free to respond to supply and demand, given time, both energy consumers and energy producers would respond in their own self-interests to price signals. These responses would result in a better state of the world than would government directives.

Any socially unacceptable resulting income inequities should then be resolved through income tax policy (windfall profits tax) rather than through energy price determination. Further controversial economic aspects of this scenario relate to how sensitive U.S. supply and demand are to price signals and whether a free-market policy is appropriate in the context of responding to sudden and sometimes noneconomically motivated actions of an international oil cartel. Early indications on both accounts are encouraging.

Free-market proponents have rejoiced at U.S. decontrol policies and project increased oil and gas supplies and decreased growth in usage. Under free-market pricing, clearer signals will be interpreted by energy users and supplying industries to better evaluate investment decisions. This will likely result, however, in lower opportunities for renewables, synthetics, and for longer range exotic sources such as ocean-thermal and satellite-power systems.

It is likely the decades of the 1980s and 1990s will still witness large markets for internal combustion cars and only small markets for renewables and synfuels. A return to normalcy is a genuine possibility in which real energy prices stabilize or fall. If events bear out the scenario, then public attention can be redirected from concern over the energy crisis to new issues of the 1980s—problems in world food and water supplies and opportunities in biotechnology and international trade. If not, then we should review the lessons events have taught us in the past and plan the future accordingly. The remainder of this book provides inputs for a better future American energy policy.

2 The Political Process and Energy

David A. Stockman

A doctor of economics and a congressman were passing through a field one day, and suddenly they stumbled into a deep hole. After they regained consciousness, the congressman looked up at a wall that ran twenty-five feet to the surface and asked the learned economist if he had a plan for getting them out. After pondering for a moment or two, the economist replied, "Well, first assume we have a ladder. . . ."

It is my contention nothing is more threatening to the future of a free and prosperous republic in these United States than the enervating symbiosis illustrated in this story. For eight years the political theater known as energy policymaking in this country has consisted of the energy professorate assuming more and more ladders of increasing implausibility, and the "can-do," fix-'em-up politicians climbing, scrambling their way up those imaginary escape routes.

Brandishing their macromodels, energy workshops, and long-term comprehensive studies, the energy professorate has introduced enough invalid assumptions and dubious premises into the intellectual marketplace in recent years to fill the Grand Canyon. A few of these are: "All of the big petroleum fields have been found," to which I would add: except for those in Mexico, Iraq, and probably some other places around. "Oil and gas production will peak in seven years"—a true proposition if measured from the publication date of the latest forecast. "The elasticity of demand for energy is low," except in the longer run. "The elasticity of energy supply is even lower," barring the development of new extraction and processing technology.

A few more theorems can be itemized without mention of the caveats put into the intellectual marketplace in recent years: (1) The marketplace is highly risk averse and will not commercialize new technologies; (2) The American people are immoral energy gluttons who will not alter their consumption habits; (3) Consumers cannot understand life-cycle costing, and energy is such a low fraction of the typical firm's input costs that it will waste fuel regardless of price; (4) Trading on the world market for our residual energy supplies is dangerous because it undermines the national security and balance of payments, increases inflation and unemployment, and causes us to lose influence even in the United Nations; (5) The law of supply and demand has been suspended until further notice—a worldwide petroleum gap will therefore appear in approximately 1985, or 1988 if we are lucky, and in no case later than 13 September 1992; and (6) A major change in the relative price of a commodity which accounts for only a minor share of the Gross National Product (GNP)—about 4 percent—will cause wrenching economic dislocations in the form of profit windfalls here, income deficits there, and output losses everywhere. Eighty years ago such mutterings would not have constituted a clear and present danger. Congress still tended to debate problems before it acted upon them. It observed certain rules and norms about appropriate and inappropriate activities by the state.

But not anymore. After four decades of indiscriminate governmental activism, Congress no longer debates or deliberates. It has become instead a legislative sausage factory. You crank in the problem, and Congress will crank out the solution—in triplicate.

Fed a steady diet of worsening false assumptions about the nation's and the world's energy condition for eight years, we have now reached a fever pitch of activity. Last year, fifty subcommittees held five thousand hours of energy hearings on 1,050 new bills pertinent thereto.

Is it any wonder the nation's energy production, distribution, and consumption systems are groaning under a deluge of orders, directives, mandates, taxes, regulations, and subsidies? Having struck the windfall-tax gusher, the federal government will displace the capital markets with a bottomless quiver of subsidies, tax credits, loan guarantees, energy security corporations, mobilization boards, government oil companies (GOCOs), solar banks, conservation banks, and just plain mountebanks.

But my congressional colleagues are not really totalitarians. There is not a collectivist bone in their bodies, nor are they romantic softheads of the soft path who believe that affluence and economic growth lead to stunted moral development, even if that is the inadvertent consequence of the present energy blitzkrieg. They are just good, conscientious men and women who have been scared by a passel of professors carrying imaginary ladders to Capitol Hill. Let me state my quarrel with the professors who initiated this mindless stampede to a Leviathan state.

In October 1973 a rather profound but straightforward event occurred that initiated a drastic reordering of the economic furniture of the entire world economy. After having increased their oil production rate by 300 percent during the previous seven years, from eight to twenty-three million barrels per day, after having satisfied nearly 90 percent of the world economy's voracious demand for additional cheap energy during the previous three years, and after having reached the limits of then-installed production capacity, the five sovereign states of the Persian Gulf apparently decided that enough was enough.

During the next seven years, they added no new production capacity. Their petroleum output more or less plateaued. The world economy consequently was confronted first with a wrenching price shock and then with the massive task of reconfiguring its entire capital stock, from automobiles to oil-field technology, to compensate for this sudden leap upward along the supply-and-demand schedules.

This task of reordering of the worldwide capital stock was so far-reaching—bearing implications for the insulation thickness of attics, the design of transmissions, the mix of industrial boiler fuels, and competitive position of natural rubber and cotton versus synthetics, residential development and commuter patterns, oil-patch discovery and recovery technologies, transportation versus extraction tradeoffs on the world's energy frontiers, among other things—that no computer model, think-tank seminar, international energy secretariat, Department of Energy or congressional subcommittee could hope to figure it out. It was a problem whose solution was tailor made almost exclusively for markets.

The First False Hypothesis

But before we had a chance to fathom this, the professors descended on Capitol Hill, dragging their ladders behind them. The first false premise peddled by the professors was the most pernicious in my view. "The world is running out of oil," Congress was told by the Ford Foundation, the MIT Workshop of Alternate Energy Sources (WAES), the Harvard Business School, and sundry others.

Obviously, no self-respecting Congress is going to let the nation's gas tank run dry. So there has been an avalanche of projects, big and small, to legislate less consumption or the quick manufacture of substitutes. Some of the big disasters will be mentioned later, but for the moment let just one small testament to the legislative power of an invalid premise suffice: Section 402 of the 1978 Industrial Powerplant and Fuel Use Act makes punishable by a fine of $500 per offense the use of natural gas for outdoor decorative lighting.

This example of a revival of the sumptuary laws is not all-encompassing since it does not include comparable fuel waste in butane lighters, model airplanes, or gaslit fireplaces. And memorial lights, or those necessary to conform to local architectural style, are exempted.

As it turns out, even that glutton for administrative minutiae, the Department of Energy, recoiled from the task of snuffing out the nation's gaslights and delegated the job to the states. Pennsylvania, Ohio, and Illinois are busy ferreting out an estimated 170,000 offending lumination devices and processing nearly five hundred petitions for exception.

What in the world is a free society, allegedly governed by rational men, doing issuing cease and desist orders to lamp posts? My answer is that its leaders have been mesmerized by bad advice.

From the beginning, the oil exhaustion hypothesis rated with the flat earth doctrine. The MIT-WAES study said that all of the big fields were gone and the reserve addition rate would plummet below the current consumption level, bringing a steady fall in proven inventories. Well, we are still waiting. During the past seven years, the free world has used cumulatively 100 billion barrels more of oil, but it has added even more, 128 billion, to reserves. Additionally, there are prodigious tar sand accumulations, coals and shales, and some allowance should be made for the expansionary effects of technology, price, and time on the six trillion barrels of oil-in-place underlying conventional reserve estimates. What about the massive lesser-grade geologic deposits—coals and shales—that are not included in the usual planetary inventory because their hydrogen-carbon ratios do not mesh well with the finished fuel specifications of 1980 industrial combustion technology? If there is any good bet, it is that the technology will change well before the resources are extinguished by unforeseeable geologic events.

Of course the exhaustion the professors were talking about never had much to do with Mother Earth subsiding into empty reservoirs. The depletion they implicitly forecast was that of human intellect, economic institutions, and our capacity for technological imagination and innovation. I regret that they failed to make that distinction clear, because while my colleagues do not know what to believe about geology, they would never have swallowed such revisionism about free men and free institutions.

The Second False Hypothesis

The next hypothesis is that there is no longer a functioning world oil market—the OPEC cartel has repealed the law of supply and demand, and it now hangs the world price from a political sky hook. Predictably, Congress set about in the home market to repeal the same economic rules that the sheiks had allegedly quashed abroad.

That is the essential rationale for the destructive network of petroleum market price controls, allocations, and entitlement subsidies that have been erected since 1973. If the world price is a politically imposed artifact, Congress reasoned, then it is too high for domestic consumers, too remunerative for domestic producers, and too remote from the real economics of energy to function as a resource allocation mechanism over that one-third share of the free-world economic activity conducted between our shores. So in ten thousand pages of regulations the Congress insulated the domestic market from the OPEC stranglehold. The question increasingly arises, however, as to who is strangling what.

I offer three results of this "false world price" assumption. First, it inexorably begat the entitlements program, as a necessary equilibrating mechanism in an economy trying to mix a shifting blend of unjustly priced foreign oil and justly priced domestic supplies. While the entitlements program indeed blended the various pricing categories, it also massacred domestic refinery investment patterns.

Since 1974 the private sector has built only one new world-scale U.S. refinery, but our government has subsidized the construction of sixty-five teapot refineries averaging 12,000 barrels per day capacity. The bottom line: massive economic waste and a few overnight Department of Energy millionaires thrown in for good measure.

Second, consider the complex bureaucratic science of crude oil categorization and pricing. This scheme will not go away with decontrol because the crude oil excise tax essentially incorporates these categories into an after-tax price structure that parallels the control system. The essential characteristic of a "just" price under this regime is that it is derived not by reference to cost, risk, or return but is a method of valuation conferred by rank of birth. There are sixteen ranks of oil and twenty-five classes of natural gas, depending on the date and circumstances of spudding, the energy equivalent of conception. Tracing the lineage of a given barrel of oil gets quite involved.

A third case concerns the gasoline shortage anomaly in ten cities in spring 1979. When requested to explain such curious developments as shortages in cities and ample supplies in the neighboring countryside, stations open 100 hours per week in New Mexico and 20 hours a week in Washington, D.C., gasoline supply availabilities of 93 percent nationwide but less than 70 percent in many retail markets, I recall that former Department of Energy administrator David Bardin gave a candid answer: " If we tried to allocate milk," he said, "we would get the same result."

Unfortunately, such candid admissions in the heat of the moment do little to deter the unfolding logic of an invalid premise. During the worst of the June 1979 gas lines, for example, a sizable minority of my colleagues was ready to fix this Department of Energy-inspired retail market disorder with an even more prodigious disorder—end-use consumer rationing.

My most poignant realization of the dangers of the OPEC price premise came during a harangue one of my colleagues delivered to a Department of Energy official for failure to enforce its antihoarding regulations. The background was this: in a controlled gasoline market that translates sudden surges in crude prices into gradual, predictable increases in product prices, the priority-user status granted to farmers and other worthies entitling them to unlimited supplies was causing a huge inventory buildup in these areas. My colleague wanted to stop the hoarding, but the Department of Energy official confessed that after four years of unstinting effort, the department had yet to arrive at a satisfactory definition of hoarding. Whereupon my colleague, without even giving it a second thought, proceeded to suggest that we license the sale of steel tanks instead, as a way of getting at the problem.

Some may think this line of causation here is farfetched, but what is really farfetched is how long the cartel premise survived as a pretext for unlimited meddling in the domestic energy markets. Among the exporters, there has never been a semblance of a coordinated production control strategy, the sine qua non for a genuine cartel. During the glut of 1978, market forces, not the OPEC secretariat, prorated production on the eminently logical basis of whose price differentials were most out of line.

During 1979 we witnessed the outbreak of a classic seller's market. Consequently, the official price structure was swamped by market forces, revealing OPEC for what it really is: an exporters' rate-publishing bureau that only functions well when it is not needed, during periods of supply-and-demand stability. And as for the assumption that high prices automatically connote artificial postings, in 1980 Egypt and the U.S. Naval Petroleum Reserve Administration were the high-price gougers on the world market at $41 per barrel.

It is critically important to understand the operation of the world market. The accurate premise is that the petroleum market is a massive world unitary system fully integrated from Tokyo to Rotterdam, and to Des Moines, too, after domestic crude prices are fully decontrolled in 1981. This system is completely arbitraged by thousands of vigilant brokers, causing it to seek a single price everywhere. It also possesses an internal short-run adjustment dynamism too powerful and unfathomable for any government, consumer, or producer to contend with effectively.

The factor that has been ignored or underrated too often by analysts is the massive above-ground inventory: nearly five billion barrels of oil in process or on hold, stretching from the export terminals, to slow- and fast-steaming tankers, to refinery tank farms and industrial storage facilities scattered around the globe. The measurement line on the dipstick of this global inventory rises and falls with the weather, money rates, the news, and a million changing psychologies, as was demonstrated during 1979 when a large part of the price increase was sustained by rapid inventory accumulation at all levels.

This churning inventory pipeline is a quintessential market process that can easily neutralize short-run intervention efforts by governments of even the biggest market participants. In April 1979, for example, the U.S. government issued three bureaucratic decrees—mandatory thermostat settings, weekend gas station closings, and emergency electric light restrictions—designed to reduce U.S. consumption by 400,000 barrels per day. The theory was that by withholding a specified amount of demand to account for the Iranian shortfall, the price adjustment could be held in check. An unexpected development occurred on the way to the predictable flood of new rules explaining when it is legitimate to have a plug-in fan on your office desk. By fall, the worldwide inventory accumulation rate had surged to perhaps two million barrels per day, thus easily overwhelming any demand effects attributable to complying office buildings.

In fairness it must be noted that Mr. Yamani's grand design of December 1979 for reunifying the oil price structure met the same fate. His logical assumption that the inventory accumulation rate would taper off and soften world demand pressures after the turn of the year was intercepted by Russian tanks moving into Afghanistan.

The point is that the world petroleum market works, even if we do not like its outcome in general or at any particular moment in time. Dogmatic insistence that it is rigid or rigged, artificial, and avoidable will not make it so. It will only encourage Congress to heap controls, entitlements, thermostat rules, wood-stove tax credits, and assorted other wasteful or coercive baggage on our domestic energy markets. To be sure, the long-run price and supply trends are worse than they would have to be in a totally enlightened world; and not every oil exporter behaves like a classic profit-maximizing firm.

Saudi Arabia, Kuwait, and the United Arab Emirates have apparently declined the invitation to double their installed production and loading capacity on the rather plausible theory that 20 million barrels leaving the straits per day and $600 million in payment entering each day is about all the region can bear. But these national investment and production policies are known and can be accounted for by all participants in the world market. They are only one factor among multiple constraints imposed on worldwide production rates by a number of parties and forces. Indeed, rather than cartel perfidy in particular, the real problem is government stupidity in general.

As examples, the Indonesians need the added revenue of high oil production to meet the requirements of a huge population. But between 1974 and 1979 they practically taxed new exploration activity out of their country. The Norwegians need some way to pay for their welfare state, but they have held down North Sea leasing and production rates on the basis of the rather curious doctrine that an increase in national wealth would be socially counterproductive. On the North American continent, the Canadian and U.S. governments have succeeded in lowering the oil and gas production rate by two to three million barrels per day by virtue of a calamitous burden of price controls and production taxes.

When all is said and done, the greatest single contributor to the present unsatisfactory supply-price balance in the world market is the monetary policy of the U.S. government. By flooding the world monetary system with excess dollars and thereby promoting the rapid depreciation of all paper currencies, we are encouraging potential exporters everywhere to believe that their petroleum reserves will appreciate faster in the ground than as claims on the world economy and inducing them to calibrate their national policies accordingly.

Thus, getting the premise right about the world market leads in a far different direction than the mushrooming bureaucratic apparatus being assembled by the Congress under the spur of the professors' horror stories about foreign oil. For example, whipped into a frenzy by the warnings of the Harvard Business School report,[1] Congress adopted the Emergency Energy Conservation Act, the most ominous extension yet of the tentacles of governmental power. Under this gem, the Department of Energy will establish gasoline consumption targets for each state for each month of the year, with all the usual adjustments for seasonality, shrimp-fishing, wheat production, and abnormal weather patterns. It will require the creation of fifty "mini-DOE's" empowered to snoop, meddle, and cavil wherever a Btu is burned; and it will enforce these arbitrary targets by plastering red, green, and yellow "no drive" stickers on the nation's windshields, closing our factories one day per week, or gas stations two, three, or even four days per week.

There is an alternative to this slide down the road to national serfdom: new policies to produce more of our indigenous energy resources and less of our national currency and liberate the inventive capacity of free men and free markets to cope with changes in the global balance of available resources.

A Third False Hypothesis

I believe that Lord Keynes was correct when he once said something like: "Madmen in authority, who hear voices in the air, are distilling their frenzy from some academic scribbler of a few years back." Nowhere is this frenzy seen more clearly than in the bureaucratic juggernaut rambling toward nationalizing the design of all consumer appliances, automobiles, homes, and buildings in this country. The polite euphemism for this power grab is mandatory energy conservation standards. Somewhere in the bowels of the Department of Energy there exists a raging debate about whether the same efficiency standard should apply to natural convection, noncleaning, solid door ovens as applies to forced convection, continuous cleaning, glass door ovens. Who started such a ludicrous altercation in the first place? Some defunct energy professor said the elasticity for energy is low, and consumers are too stupid to understand the intricacies of life-cycle costing.

The last seven years have laid that theorem to rest decisively. Despite the underpricing of natural gas and oil, U.S. energy consumption per dollar of real economic activity declined from 61,000 Btus in 1973 to 50,000 Btus in 1979, a 17 percent reduction. For the industrial world as a whole, consumption has declined by the equivalent of six million barrels energy equivalent daily, relative to the pre-1973 GNP energy ratios.

Of course, the short-run elasticity of demand for energy is quite low, primarily because a sow's ear cannot be transformed into a silk purse overnight. But over time, the capital stock does adjust in response to changed relative prices, just as economists used to believe. Moreover, consumers learn faster than professors ever thought. The best way to learn about life-cycle costing of automobiles, for instance, is to try to trade in a 1977 Buick Le Sabre. The blue book does not explain the theory; it just records the huge drop in value due to the doubling of gasoline prices, and it has also encouraged more than a few buyers to purchase gasoline-efficient cars.

Unfortunately, while the empirical evidence rolls in, the mandatory efficiency statutes bump and grind toward implementation. In the case of the appliance law, for example, the statute specified thirteen standards for such categories as ranges, refrigerators, air conditioners, and automatic dishwashers. But it now appears that the inherent fuel consumption characteristics of natural gas versus electric appliances require separate standards; and major utility features such as self-cleaning ovens, glass doors, burner element size, number of rinse cycles, and through-the-door ice dispensers also create wide disparities requiring separate standards. The bottom line is that we are all going to have to buy standardized, minimum-utility, government-issue toasters, or we are going to have 50, 100, or 300 separate appliance efficiency standards. The outrageous part of this development is not the Kafkaesque nature of the whole enterprise, but what it will do to consumers and producers alike. Low-priced models of everything will disappear from the market as consumer considerations of purchase cost, utilization patterns, and utility characteristics give way to the sumptuary goals of the standards writers.

Unfortunately, the appliance saga is only a minor chapter in this whole madness. The next shoe to fall is called BEPS (Building Energy Performance Standards), wherein a mandatory, annual Btu diet will be prescribed for every new building in the land. For each of twenty-one categories of structure types, one will multiply a fixed energy consumption factor times the square footage, and with formula variations for heating and cooling degree-days in the locale, derive the permissible annual fuel consumption down to the last gallon, cubic foot, or kilowatt hour. Consider the implications for the single-family dwelling, where the rule says x units of energy per square foot of interior space—period. Some people prefer bay windows and some shuttered double-hung; some prefer fireplaces, sauna baths, and high ceilings, and others low ceilings and large recreation rooms; some prefer to perch atop a hillside facing west and others to snuggle at the bottom facing east; some want darkrooms, some want sunrooms. In the brave new world of BEPS you may have to install a solar-activated heat pump in order to keep your bay window in the blueprint.

The Fourth False Hypothesis

Obviously, the passage of time is taking its toll on many of the ladders hauled to Washington just a few years ago. But it has not slowed down the energy professors or deterred the invention of new and even more implausible assumptions. The most ominous at the moment is the "overdependency" thesis that Professors Stobaugh and Yergin have so tirelessly disseminated. That particular ladder is unleashing more legislative mayhem than any single idea that has gone before. Why, for example, are we imposing a draconian $230 billion production tax on domestic oil and gas producers over the next decade? Primarily because the Congress has been convinced that it needs new revenues to subsidize the creation of a synfuels industry and to finance a potpourri of credits, grants, and loans to encourage the purchase of conservation devices.

In order to stimulate the frontiers of new technology, tax credits will be offered for wood stoves, residential coal furnaces, portable radiant heaters, windmills, and heat pumps. To accelerate the retrofit of existing housing stock, we will mandate the transformation of our most inefficient economic institutions—gas and electric utilities—into vendors of building audits, building contractors, and home improvement lenders. We will further encourage them to scatter their capital base across the entire countryside by buying insulation and solar collectors, installing these items without charge, and recovering their investment capital via amortization charges to their customers. For good measure, they will be encouraged to redistribute a goodly amount of income according to essentially Monte Carlo principles by rate-basing low-interest loans and charging one and all equally—the owner of the mansion and the bungalow, the homeowner who bought his own insulation three years ago, and the procrastinator who waited for somebody else to do it today.

There is no telling, of course, what the $88 billion Energy Security Corporation will produce, but it is not likely to produce much fuel at any time soon. Commercialization of new energy technologies is not one of the government's strong suits, if current Department of Energy activities in this field are any guide.

The Department of Energy, for example, has funded research in fluorescent lights, textile loom efficiency, tire reclamation, high-frequency hand tools, low-energy cement, and a host of similar areas. According to documents recently submitted to the Energy and Power Subcommittee on which I serve, some bureaucrat has gotten so enthralled in doing Goodyear's laboratory work and product development he is now forecasting a savings of 10,000 barrels per day of energy in the year 2000 due to the accelerated use of recycled tires stemming from his efforts. I would only note that even the Communist bloc countries gave up this kind of materials balance planning some decades ago.

Concluding the Overdependency Thesis

The first assumption is that overdependency threatens our national security. My answer is that Soviet tanks and planes are what threaten our national security, and the enactment of wood-stove tax credits or no-drive days at home will not slow their advance a bit.

To use a metaphor, this whole argument confuses the massive deposits in the bank vault with the relatively miniscule daily rate of withdrawal. The hydrocarbons in the Persian Gulf geologic vault are worth $30 trillion at 1980 prices. Soviet annexation would devastate the economic foundations of the entire free world, regardless of whether America's much maligned automobile drivers were using 7, 4, or 2 million barrels of gasoline per day at whatever time the Soviet tanks roll across the Iranian border or the Saudi princes are shot in a midnight coup. National security has traditionally been purchased through the defense budget, a tradition I believe we would be well advised to continue. There remains the lesser threat of regional instability, change of regimes, and temporary production interruptions. But if properly assessed, these threats hardly should be cause for energy isolationism achieved by inundating our home economy with an ever-expanding bureaucratic amoeba.

During 1979, for example, the Iranians exchanged a twentieth-century regime for a seventh-century one, and their production declined three million barrels a day. The Iraqis, on the other hand, purged their regime, altered their domestic and international policies, and increased production by 1.5 million barrels per day, with some reports indicating production levels of up to 5 million barrels per day by 1985. Similarly, when the United States embargoed Iranian oil in 1979, the tanker traffic was rerouted, exactly as would have happened if Nigeria had embargoed shipments to the United States last summer, as it threatened during a miff over our Rhodesian policies. To be sure, a change of regimes in Saudi Arabia, a regional Middle East war, or the outbreak of commando sabotage could interrupt the Persian Gulf flow for a sustained period of time. But the questions are for how long and how do you insure against it?

Marxist sentries faithfully guarding Gulf Oil Company's production platforms in Angola suggest that even radicals and non-Caucasians recognize the value of oil export sales and that sustained production outages consequently are not likely. For the shorter term interruptions, an industrial world strategic storage system of 2 to 3 billion barrels that might be financed for a few cents in annual insurance premium charges, could cover even a Saudi outage for up to two years. In short, the recitation of coups, plagues, and typhoons does not particularly validate the argument.

Aside from national security, the overdependency thesis relies mostly on economic mirrors. It is said that we cannot sustain the burden of financing current oil import levels. That proposition, in my view, is a mercantilist heresy, pure and simple. We can afford to finance whatever amount of imported oil, Toyotas, and transistor radios our people choose to buy, so long as they are generating the real income necessary to pay for them. The problem with our balance of payments and our currency value does not stem from too many tankers lined up at our ports, but from too many dollars being pushed out of the open market desk by the Federal Reserve Board and too large a tax wedge being levied on domestic production by the Congress.

Finally, the overdependency thesis contains a price theory that borders close to economic alchemy. The proposition is that if Congress turned down the U.S. oil consumption spigot by, say, 1.5 million barrels per day, this would have the salutary effect of lowering the world price, reducing our import bill, and incidentally helping our friends in Japan reduce the cost of making cars and machine tools.

Unfortunately, the economic windfall has been calculated in gross rather than in net national terms. We have to add back in the subsidy cost of wood-stove credits, solar collectors, and the lost output from some of the more coercive consumption-control measures that have been proposed to implement this strategy.

More importantly, such purported economic savings will occur if and only if nothing else of consequence changes on a planet inhabited by 4 billion human beings. The price gains postulated will obviously never materialize, for example, if some sheik in Kuwait decides to turn down the production spigot by an equal 1.5 millions barrels per day; or they will not materialize if in response to an initially lower price consumers in South Korea, West Germany, and Brazil increase their consumption by 1.5 million barrels per day over time; or if on the margin some nomad in Ethiopia gets off his camel and starts driving a jeep.

Note

1. Robert Stobaugh and Daniel Yergin, eds., *Energy Future: The Report of the Harvard Business School Energy Project* (New York: Random House, 1979).

Questions and Answers to Part I

Question: Are there any areas of legitimate market failure where government intervention is desirable; if so, what are those areas and what should be the nature of the intervention?

Answer: A major area of market failure we have totally ignored is the matter of storage. We need a strategic storage system managed by the government, financed in terms of operating costs and maintenance costs by a small levy on each barrel of imported oil, and insurance premium. The acquisition cost of the oil obviously should be bond financed since oil in the ground will appreciate over time and will generate more than enough income to pay off the bonds as well as the interest rate. If we had this kind of large strategic inventory build up, done on an OECD (Organization of Economic Cooperation and Development) or international basis, then when a production outage occurred, oil could be released at some set rate into the market. We would not have fears and worry on the part of the American public and panic on the part of Congress to adopt all kinds of wild mechanisms to do something about it—when usually those mechanisms do not get into place until after the market is restabilized. A strategic program would be far better than gasoline rationing or no-drive days or closing the stations or many of the other silly things proposed in 1979, including gasoline consumption targets state by state.

Question: Do we need government requirements on the information that has to be made available to people who make decisions?

Answer: Yes. I do not have nearly as big a problem with disclosure, information labeling, and that sort of thing as I have with the mandatory efficiency standards and like bureaucratic efforts to alter consumption patterns through rigid rules. We must remember that consumers have ways of getting information that some of us sophisticates have never even thought about. Information is generated in plenty of ways; it is much more informal, it is much harder to fathom and trace than a lot of us imagine, but in some cases additional information, I think, would be helpful.

Question: The traditional method of regulating rates where there is a clear natural monopoly, that is, in transmission and distribution of electricity and also natural gas, is based upon rolled-in average cost pricing where the capital charges are evidence more of the cost of five, or ten, or fifteen years ago than today's costs. Isn't the decision maker comparing past costs of the centralized energy supply with current costs of either decentralized supply options or energy efficiency improvement options?

Answer: I used to advocate marginal cost pricing everywhere, until I started to examine the difference between a private firm in a competitive market and a regulated monopoly utility. There are two problems: (1) marginal cost pricing initially generates revenues far in excess of what the rate of return ceiling on a regulated utility would permit; then (2) How should those extra revenues be used without getting into basic income redistribution? If we can solve these problems, then I might be interested in trying to do something about marginal cost pricing for monopolies.

Question: If you openly deal with marginal cost pricing, you invite the question of subsidizing investments on energy consumption and you have to address that balance. And you have problems if you do not address the matter of equal cost pricing.

Answer: It is basically a problem in electricity. On natural gas, we should have deregulated the field price years ago. Once we get full deregulation, the purchase or acquisition price of the natural gas utility will be a market price that will pass through, and the consumer will face the marginal cost at all times. We are about eight years away from that. On electricity, I can not see any way that it can be done.

Question: The Department of Energy and the whole energy program seem to have been designed so far to support the OPEC cartel. It is almost as if the U.S. government is a partner of that cartel at the present time. I am talking in the general context of reducing U.S. supplies, increasing demands, and so forth.

Answer: Right. We do not support the cartel, just an unnecessarily high world price that everybody takes advantage of.

Question: Exactly. Now, given that the United States is an official partner through the windfall profits tax, in addition to income tax, do you think there's any reasonable chance that the price of oil could go down in real terms?

Answer: Anybody in the business of predicting the price of oil in 1982 to 1985 or 1990 ought to read the major reports that have been made since 1974. He will find everybody—whether it is industry, academia, or government—has been so wrong, even in horizons of three to four years, that we should avoid that game. And when you see reports from Department of Energy, making forecasts for 1995 and the year 2000, by sector, broken down by fuel, you have to wonder whether we are living in a fictional world or a real world.

Question: You have blamed a lot on the economic professors. Is it really all their fault?

Answer: Yes, in a way it is. I spent two weeks last summer in a conference with four or five senators, five or six members of the House, writing the Emergency Energy Conservation Act of 1979. There are those in Congress who do not believe in prices, markets, supply and demand, and who believe we ought to have a bureaucratically managed economy, so they were all for this. But they are not a majority; they are a minority.

Nevertheless, the fact that we wrote this bill was primarily due to the moderates—sensible, open-minded, middle-of-the-road Democrats—who came to the conference carrying the report of the Harvard Business School, saying that we have to do something to conserve. Now I do not know whether Professor Yergin meant that we ought to have gasoline consumption targets for all states of the union every month adjusted for shrimp fishermen, and so forth. Nevertheless, his implication, his policy recommendation, was to conserve drastically in order to bring down that import level from 8 to 6 million barrels per day, as if that would make any difference.

Some people are very cynical, and they think legislation is all politics, power-block maneuvering, making trades. That is not so. Ideas have a large impact, and if they are wrong, then the policies, the programs, the regulations, the activity at the governmental level that flow from them can have disastrous consequences.

Question: You were saying that a cut-off of supply from the Persian Gulf was unlikely unless because of interdiction by Russians.

Answer: No, I am saying there are two cases: the Soviet intervention case, which we have to prevent regardless of whether we are getting any oil there; or the local instability case, which we can handle through a combination of strategic storage and recognizing these interruptions as unlikely to persist for a long period of time.

Question: We are currently trying to guess what the Department of Energy is going to issue within its petroleum contingency allocation planning. It looks as though we will face, say, the total with the International Energy Agency obligation around ten million barrels a day available for North

America instead of twenty million barrels a day, assuming the Persian Gulf gets cut off completely.

So, my question, as a policy issue, is how large a storage capability, how draconian an allocation policy in the country should be made, and how quickly can it be put in place?

Answer: Yes, that is the worst contingency—the Persian Gulf entirely closed and nothing comes out for months. It is a low-order contingency, but one we have to plan for and think about.

To draw the conclusion that the United States, and indeed the entire western world, ought to withdraw purchases or drastically scale back purchases from the Persian Gulf and replace them with much higher cost domestic home-canned production or with conservation does not make sense. So then, how do we deal with that? I made some calculations. A 2- or 3-billion barrel strategic storage reserve—and I am not talking just about the United States, but also Japan, OECD, and Western Europe—would not be an insurmountable reserve system to create over a period of a couple of years. We should have started in 1975. I am talking about 3 billion barrels in excess of the working-level lubricants we need in the vast pipeline that keeps the refineries running and the tankers moving and the distribution system going.

You could finance that very cheaply with an insurance premium of less than a dollar a barrel. Persian Gulf oil is cheaper than everything else around and our economies will be better off if we use that versus high-cost substitutes. That seems to me an eminently sensible bargain; but, unfortunately, there has been no interest in successive administrations at Department of Energy or in the Congress because the alternative is really much more fun for politicians. In a 10-million-barrel-a-day outage you can start ordering everybody around, allocating gasoline, allocating crude oil among refineries, managing the distribution system, putting out blue, red, and yellow stickers. All kinds of exercises of power are possible. We do not want to think about a strategic storage because the market can then pretty well handle the allocation distributions.

Question: I understand the House is considering the establishment of an energy committee. I would like to know your attitude on that?

Answer: Two comments. This proposal, pending in the House, does not consolidate any energy jurisdiction whatever, except for some minor things regarding the Interior committee. Basically, what it does is take the Energy and Power Subcommittee of Commerce, elevate it to full committee status, create six more energy subcommittees therefore in the House, triple the size of the staff and probably the budget. That would mightily exacerbate the problem we already have with too much legislation and too much intervention. I think it is a bad idea.

On a more practical, technical level, if you wanted to have a centralized energy committee, and there might be something to be said for that just in terms of efficiency, and so forth, the best way is to take the energy jurisdiction that flows from the three committees. Commerce, Banking, Currency, and Ways and Means: Commerce directly, the other two through the tax and financing tools that fall within their committees.

Question: The fourth branch of government—the bureaucratic agencies—go on forever. Does not the Congress have an obligation to look at their own stepchild and tell them whether or not they are moving in the right direction?

Answer: I agree with you completely. I was not trying to exonerate the Congress. We passed every one of these enabling acts that caused the Department of Energy to write efficiency standards for houses and cars, for setting up the gasoline consumption target programs. Nevertheless, we do not have any consensus in Congress about the best solution to that problem, which is to repeal the statute. A good proportion of the members think that these statutes, as difficult as the administrative problems are, such as the glass oven door versus the solid oven door, have to go forward anyway and that we have to grin and bear it because some computer model suggests this is going to help conserve some energy.

We are going to continue to have all these programs that are such serious economic wastes, to say nothing of threats to the basic nature of a free society, until we convince people that the pricing mechanism is the dynamism of markets. Substitution and technological change in response to price have worked historically, not only in energy, but in every other resource that is derived from the planet. Congress will pass the laws; then we will rant and rave at the bureaucracies that implement them when they lead to absurdly detailed results. But that is the kind of bind that we are in today unless we change the model, the assumptions, and the world view about this whole energy problem.

**Part II
Social Implications of
Energy Policies**

Introduction to Part II

Eddie N. Williams

The social implications of energy policies is a subject that often receives short shrift when developing energy policies, with more time being devoted to other complex political, economic, and international issues. And yet, it is important to have social concerns in mind and know seriously and honestly what values we have for shaping the development of energy policies.

Social implications, like other aspects of energy, obviously are very complex. We are talking about people and equity and immediately confront a problem of definitions. Equity is very hard to define. A conference produced in 1979 by the Joint Center for Political Studies began with a statement, "Equity is like love; everybody knows its meaning and everyone's meaning is different, yet its virtues are consistently praised." What is equity? It is an important question to be addressed in dealing with social implications.

Nevertheless, there is at least an intuitive consensus that equity ought to mean formulating policies to improve the condition of those who are most disadvantaged. At the minimum, equity should mean that the poor and other disadvantaged persons not be placed at a greater disadvantage. There is justifiable concern about the poor. Poor households, as a group, use considerably less energy than those whose members are well-off. They usually pay more per unit for the energy they use, and their energy bills place a heavy and growing strain on limited household budgets.

Yet we know that equity considerations extend beyond income and race to environmental concerns, employment, and a host of other quality-of-life issues; thus, identifying and resolving social consequences of our energy policies is indeed an urgent and complex matter.

3 Technology in an Information Society

John Naisbitt

We are in an increasingly complex society in which we are going to make some judgments about energy and energy technology. And the technologies we adopt in the future must be compatible with and conditioned by the emerging social and political environment. Some of the dominant changes in that environment are: (1) the shift from a mass industrial society to an information society; (2) the shift from centralization to decentralization in this society; (3) the shift from a representative democracy to a participatory democracy; and (4) the duality of the direction that society is going in—something I call "high-tech/high-touch."

Information Society

We have moved and are moving from a mass industrial society to an information society, and the changes involved will easily be as profound as those that occurred when we moved from an agricultural society to an industrial society.

According to census data, at the turn of the century, 35 percent of us were in industrial occupations; 35 percent of us were also in agricultural occupations, which has dropped to 4 percent. In 1950, 65 percent of us were in industrial occupations. Since 1950, that has dropped to 30 percent—a remarkable change. Since 1950, 17 percent of us were in information occupations, which has now gone up to more than 54 percent. More than half of us are in the information industry.

We have been told that the postindustrial society is going to be a service society. But we did not notice that all the growth in the service sector was with regard to information. The service sector, minus information occupations, is about 11 or 12 percent, as it has been for decades. That does not change. (The character of service jobs changes. There are few domestics these days, but there are many people in fast food businesses.) The postindustrial society is clearly an information society.

Since we were mostly farmers in 1800, an agricultural way of life structured American society in many ways that began to work poorly as we entered a mass industrial society. What we did during the long period as a mass industrial society is now increasingly unsuitable as we shift into an information society. Not long ago the number one occupation in the United States became clerk, for the first time, succeeding laborer, succeeding farmer, representing a short history of the United States. Someone asked me what comes after clerk. I do not know whether it will be poet or soldier, but probably by the end of the century we will know. So those mass social instrumentalities created during the industrial period are getting more and more out of tune. Labor unions are on the long irreversible downward slide. National political parties exist in name only today. Network television is similarly on the decline.

In a mass industrial society the strategic resource is capital. In an information society, the strategic resource is information, experience, knowhow. Shifting from capital as the strategic resource to information means access to the economic system is much easier. And what you would expect to happen is happening. There is an explosion of entrepreneurial activity in the United States.

The time orientation in an agricultural society is the past: we learn from the past how to plant and harvest. The time orientation in an industrial society is the present: now, ad hoc, get it out. The time orientation in an information society is the future. We have to learn from the future in precisely the ways we have been learning from the past.

Decentralization

About three years ago we started decentralizing our society more than we continued to centralize. The two great profound centralizing phenomena in this country were the Great Depression and World War II, plus the centralizing impact of industrialization. We are now receding from all three and are celebrating diversity in this society more and more. In the 1950s we started to celebrate individual diversity. In the 1960s we started to celebrate ethnic diversity. A phenomenon of the 1970s was the beginning of the celebration of jurisdictional diversity, and the almost chauvinistic regionalism that has been expressed recently and will become more and more striking (particularly in connection with have and have-not energy states) is part of this geographic diversity.

We do not have a national urban policy in the United States today because the old master plan, top-down kind of national policy is out of tune. It is inappropriate to ask, "Are we going to save our cities?" That is an either/or formulation in an increasingly multiple-option society. We are going to save some of our cities; we are not going to save others. We are going to save some a little; we are going to save some quite a bit; and it is going to turn on local initiative. The only national urban policy that is in tune with the times is the one responsive to local initiative, and that is true of energy, health, and many other things.

There has been a shift from the presidency to the Congress, and, less noticed, from the Congress to the states. While we will see less federal regulation, we will see more state regulation. We will see more incentiveness on behalf of localities in the states as we move from an essentially centralized society to a profoundly decentralized society. That is well under way.

Participating Democracy

We created a representative society when we needed to be represented. We elected people who went off to Washington and represented us and came back and told us what went on. Now, with instantaneously shared information, we know almost as much about what is going on as some of our representatives, and in many cases, a lot more. We do not need that kind of representation when we have instantaneously shared information. That is part of the reason we moved to more participatory democracy.

Another part of the phenomenon is a shift from party politics to issue politics. Similarly, we are doing away with the large general-purpose instrumentalities. An early and easy example of this are the general-purpose magazines, with their circulations of millions, *Life*, *Look*, and *Post*, which failed about a decade ago. At the same time we created several hundred special-interest magazines. We now have several thousand special-interest publications, and no general-purpose magazines.

That is the analogue. The American Medical Association is getting weaker while structures within it are getting stronger: the psychiatrists and brain surgeons, the county organizations, and so forth. The National Association of Manufacturers and the Chamber of Commerce of the United States, two umbrella organizations, announced several years ago they were going to merge for all kinds of wonderful reasons, none of which was true. They were merging for survival. A year later, they announced they were not completing the merger. Now, presumably they will die separately.

Here is another example: network television is on a long downward slide. ABC, NBC, and CBS are the *Life*, *Post*, and *Look* of the 1980s. Their audiences will be drained away by cable, video disc, and special networks—older people's network, Spanish network, BBC in America, sports network (sports twenty-four hours a day, seven days a week—terrific for what is left of the fabric of the American family).

This analogue also applies to leadership. We do not have any great captains of industry anymore, great university presidents, great leaders in the arts, great politicians. Followers create leaders and we followers are not creating those kinds of leaders any more. We are creating leaders along narrower bounds and closer proximity.

By the time California's tax-saving Proposition 13 came along it was a subset of a larger trend, a kind of direct democracy, which the Swiss invented about a hundred years ago. The culmination of direct democracy was Proposition 15 in California, where the citizens voted on whether or not to allow a nuclear plant to be built. We had never submitted questions of construction (of any sort) to the political process before, and we are more and more going to submit such questions to the political process. In connection with energy, particularly nuclear energy, we are going to do nothing in this country without submitting referenda to the people whose lives are affected by it.

High-Tech/High-Touch

In American society the introduction of any high technology seems to be accompanied by a kind of rebalancing, a compensatory human response, or the technology will be rejected. And that is true if it is in your office, home, or in the larger environment. For example, the introduction of television society was accompanied by the group therapy movement, and then the personal growth movement, and the human potential movement, much of which started in California. The lock-step development of those two phenomena is amazing.

The high technology of chemistry and pharmacology gave us "the pill," which really led to a revolution in life-styles, moving us from an either/or choice to a multiple-option society. We are more and more a multiple-option society. Formerly, we either got married or we did not. Now there is a great array of options.

The high technology of life-sustaining equipment in our hospitals has led to a concern about the quality of death and the hospices movement. Heart transplants and brain scanners led to new interest in family doctors and neighborhood clinics. The high technology of word processing in offices has led to a revival of handwritten notes and letters. (Jet airplanes, as far as I can tell, have only led to more conferences and business meetings.)

Notice the rebalancing. We have to keep that in mind with all of our solutions. So in connection with what we do about energy, we have to be aware of these overarching macrotrends that are reshaping and restructuring our society. We are not going to rebuild our world in a vacuum. Unlike the days of the technological imperative, political and social events are going to be dominant in our planning.

So it is going to be a very complicated society. We are very deeply engaged in the process of restructuring from an industrial to an information society. We are decentralizing. We are going to become an increasingly high-touch society as we continue to push high-tech. We will be a multiple-option society. We will be a much more entrepreneurial society; in short, a more complicated, perhaps even painful and uncertain, society; but, I think, a much more interesting, creative, and richer society.

4

The NAACP's Interest in Energy Policies

Margaret Bush Wilson

I approach the subject of social implications of energy policies with a circumscribed perspective and a particular bias. The circumscribed perspective grows out of years of struggle in the Civil Rights movement and from my predeliction for thinking first about protecting and preserving and enhancing human life. And so while some address the problems of inflation and slow growth, I will be discussing the pervasive impact of the problems of unemployment and poverty.

My particular bias is much more direct, and I put it bluntly: with regard to public policy and the range of alternatives from which to forge a mix that adequately meets our needs, I have one overriding concern. Namely, that no course of action on the part of this nation, or any forces in it, places any additional burden on the backs of black Americans, because I think we carry enough.

Dr. Harold Agnew, a former director of the Los Alamos Scientific Laboratory, once said: "We all wish to improve the quality of our life, but in a finite world with finite resources, until man with all his ingenuity is able to redirect some of his energies and talents to allow this qualitative improvement for all to take place, we cannot expect that in improving the lot of many, the quality for some in certain areas will not be degraded."

I present the argument that the social implications of energy policies provide the seeds of opportunity and the energy dilemmas we face can be the portent for a new frontier of progress for ourselves and our society.

NAACP under Media Fire

The National Association for the Advancement of Colored People (NAACP) came under considerable fire from the media in 1978. It received sharp criticism for "meddling in energy" from those who said that this is a field too complex and highly specialized for the purview of a civil rights organization.

This was a major challenge, for we were out to prove that minorities and the poor and other socially oriented groups have a vested interest in energy policy, beyond concern about the cost of heating fuel and the price of gasoline at the pumps. Central to the NAACP's much publicized energy statement was concern that any national energy policy that would restrict vigorous economic growth and thus reduce job opportunities for minorities was unacceptable.

Our statement called for the development of all forms of energy—solar, geothermal, biomass, off-shore oil, shale, synthetic fuels from coal, as well as nuclear—because we felt that the key to future needs is a suitable energy mix that will afford an adequate supply of energy. The central thrust of the NAACP's policy statement was, and is, that the national government must lead in assuring that the country develops abundant, affordable energy supplies that will promote vigorous economic growth. We continue to stand firmly behind that statement.

There is a caveat that I believe some will not admit, others choose to ignore, and some disregard. It is, however, a caveat that has been validated over the years, in spite of ourselves. This litmus test of American society is that the American spirit ebbs and flows and soars and stumbles on the simple test of how the nation treats its minority citizens. And today what is needed most by minorities, and particularly black Americans, is economic advancement. Or, to say it another way, more and better jobs, higher earning power, and more business opportunities.

What we in the NAACP continue to ask is: How can policies and strategies be shaped to stimulate growth, increase employment, protect the environment, and lower inflation? What we perceive is that our problems at home are linked to similar problems abroad. We are confronted with a global interdependence that suggest that the resolution of the economic ills of an industrial nation like ours may very well depend to a larger degree than ever before on the growth and prosperity of the developing nations.

Developed Countries Interrelated to Developing Countries

A number of factors suggest that the trade and financial links between the industrialized northern countries and the less developed southern countries have reached such proportions that economic conditions in the less-developed countries have a direct impact on conditions in developed countries like ours. For example, U.S. trade dependence is growing. In 1977, American exports to the non-OPEC developing countries was about 27 percent of total U.S. exports. But this is very interesting. This 27 percent was more than the combined purchases of the European community, eastern Europe, the Soviet Union, and China. And some 25 percent of U.S. imports comes from these countries.

Second, debt, which is growing in these less developed countries, stood at about $200 billion in 1980, up 84 percent since 1972. This greatly increased debt of the developing countries and their resultant need to continue to grow and expand in order to handle the repayment of that debt is another example of why the relationship between growth and progress in the developing countries and the developed countries has become so significant.

Third, the prices of various commodities and raw materials have been of great concern to rich countries since the price shocks of the early 1970s, but they have been of concern to the poor countries for a considerably longer period. Both developing and developed countries have come to understand that effective commodity agreements could be of substantial benefit to industrial as well as developing countries.

These three sets of problems—trade, commodities, debt and financing—are interrelated, and none of them can be dealt with individually. The self-interest of industrial countries like ours lies in making sure that a growing amount of financial resources from a variety of sources is available to the developing countries. Both trade measures and stable commodity prices, as well as continued access to credit from a variety of private and governmental sources, will be important in providing these resources.

Equally important will be continued financial support from the international financial institutions and an increase in bilateral and multilateral development assistance. The assertion that developing-country growth will affect developed-country well-being is supported by a recent report for the United Nations Conference on Trade and Development prepared by economists from the University of Pennsylvania. This report concludes that an increase of three percentage points in the growth rates of the non-oil exporting countries could result in an increase of one percentage point, or the equivalent of $45 billion, in the growth rates of the OECD developed countries, which includes the United States.[1]

Over a five-year period in the United States this increase could mean a gain of at least $225 billion in gross national product and a correspondingly large increase in employment. For the next decade, the interest of the developed countries in the progress and well-being of the developing countries stems from the need to address the interrelated problems of global economic stagnation, including inflation and unemployment, slower growth rate, rising protectionism, fluctuating commodity prices, and a growing debt and financing problem.

However, there is a long-term benefit that cannot be ignored. Between now and the turn of the century, three crucial problems could be addressed collaboratively by developed and developing countries, namely: food, population, and energy. With respect to energy, there is a collision course between a reliance on petroleum-based energy to achieve the world's development goals and the decline in world oil production that most experts claim will take place before the end of the century.

I maintain that a collaborative developed/developing country strategy would entail adopting energy policies that do not rely so heavily on scarce petroleum supplies, thus moving us directly to the postpetroleum energy technology of the future. Over the long run this approach would involve less reliance on nonrenewable sources of energy and greater emphasis on new and alternate sources of energy here and abroad. In this case, the developed countries have a preponderance of the capital and technical skills and the developing countries have a large supply of primary solar energy, unlimited needs for energy, and lower research costs.

If we want the benefits of liberalized trade policies that are essential and crucial to this process, we must be willing to assist trade. Displaced workers in the United States who may temporarily suffer the impact of competition from foreign imports require protection; therefore, adequate adjustment assistance must be part of any policy aimed at trade liberalization.

The NAACP Mission

The primary concern in the NAACP for developing an energy policy statement and focusing on the economic relationship between the developed and the developing countries and the potential inherent in a new international economic order is in searching for ways to make the economy work for the benefit of all of us—the fortunate as well as the least fortunate. Having embarked on this mission, we were pleasantly surprised to discover that we had won new allies in the unlikeliest places. Indeed, I had one commentator suggest that there was an oil man in the NAACP woodpile.

People have suddenly recognized that the general stability and prosperity of this nation serve to promote common interests among many groups, including the energy industries, corporations, and the civil rights organizations. Historically, we in the NAACP have had a mission in society: seeking to win the broadest possible support of a moral as well as practical rightness of justice and equality of opportunity for all. The basic reality on which we seek broad understanding is that no person or group lives in isolation. Our interests, no matter how seemingly unrelated, converge at one or several points in the daily pursuit of our respective activities. Furthermore, not only do the interests of Americans of all incomes and races and ethnic origins frequently converge, the survival of our nation is more than ever interrelated and dependent on developments beyond our national shores over which we have little control.

Note

1. Thomas Naff, ed., *The Middle East Challenge, 1980-1985* (Carbondale: Southern Illinois University Press, 1981).

5 Consumers and Energy Prices

L. Calvin Moore

Low-income families have often had to make decisions as to whether they would eat or have heat. This is a true testament of neither our technology nor our development of policies relative to energy matters. But it has necessitated considerable social activity. Various community agencies have bonded themselves together for the purpose of asking their state legislative bodies to develop laws and injunctive procedures that would prevent utility companies from shutting off heat or services for low-income people.

Entities such as the Massachusetts Fair Share Program and the Citizen-Labor Energy Coalition have been very effective in gaining the ear of those who make these policies so that they will understand the tremendous hardship that has been placed on this society. Congress has also reacted to the complaints of the American people. The Ninety-sixth Congress speedily passed a law that would provide assistance for those people who would suffer, primarily the elderly and the poor. However, since it was not a severe winter that year, the true meaning of that assistance has not been realized yet.

Thus, we need to tie in two factors: (1) high energy cost has been one of the most visible means changing the life-styles of low- and middle-income people; and (2) we must evaluate or at least determine what may have brought this about.

Impact of High Energy Prices

In a not too surprising report early in 1980, a congressional committee, investigating the rapid rise in energy costs, revealed that the price of heating oil alone had increased by 800 percent. The report also indicated that there was no justifiable reason for such an increase.[1] According to Congressman Moffett, when he spoke on the matter of deregulating petroleum products, deregulation was supposed to result in a competitive situation that would act much in the same manner as the deregulation of the airline industry. It turned out to be just the opposite, for in this case it has brought about an escalation of product prices.

When we deregulate an industry and adhere to the adage of supply and demand, it is reasonable to assume that prices would go down if the oil or petroleum industry were allowed to have those regulations removed so they could operate in a free, open, competitive society. But I concur that the policies and regulations of those involved with the Department of Energy to a great extent have affected this process.

To better understand how we have come to be in this situation, we should analyze what has happened over the past years. Since OPEC seized control of oil in 1973, three things have happened: (1) prices of gasoline, heating oil, and natural gas, coal, and electricity have gone skyward; (2) increases in consumer oil prices are much greater than increases in OPEC prices; (3) profits of oil companies have become astronomical. How were the companies able to get away with it?

How Oil Companies Benefit Themselves

You create shortages, natural gas cutoffs, and gasoline lines. Then you talk ominously about dwindling energy resources. When Congress decontrolled the price of natural gas in 1979, strangely and suddenly there were no more shortages. Since then, the gas companies have been looking for more customers, and also your gas bill continues to rise. This is an illustration of the social effects of a national energy policy.

There were gas lines of 1979. Gasoline lines simply meant customers were so anxious to get gasoline that they did not notice the price. During the 1979 gasoline shortages, the oil industry and former Secretary of Energy Schlesinger talked about crude oil shortages because of the Iranian shortfall. What were the facts? There was no Iranian shortfall. The non-Communist world production of crude oil increased by more than 5 percent in 1979 compared to that of 1978. Imports of oil into the United States last spring increased by 9 percent over the same time in 1978. Stocks of crude oil were growing throughout the period of alleged shortage.

The critical fact is that there was a refinery slow down, starting in January of 1979. Refineries operated at less than 85 percent of capacity in the spring of 1979; this is down from 90 percent in the fall of 1978. If gasoline is not being refined, shortages will result. That is exactly what happened.

An analysis of figures issued by the Department of Energy shows that refiners' margin for home heating oil increased from 7 percent per gallon in 1978 to 19.4 percent per gallon in September of 1979, an increase of 177 percent. The refiner's profits on home heating oil rose from 1.6 percent per gallon to 14.5 percent per gallon, an increase of 806 percent.

For comparison, total labor costs for refining gasoline are less than one cent per gallon. Oil workers' wages could be doubled for an additional one cent at the gas pump. This is to be kept in mind when the major oil companies start complaining they are unable to meet wage demands of workers during even the current negotiations with the Oil, Chemical and Atomic Workers International Union.

The huge increase in refiners' margins within the space of only one year must also be kept in mind when we look at the increase in our cost of living. Inflation on all items in wage earners' budgets is now rising at an annual rate of 14 percent. The energy part of the budget is inflating at 43 percent. This includes all energy items—oil, gas, coal, electricity—but oil leads the list. The oil companies and the Carter administration repeatedly stated that we must begin paying "real costs" for scarce energy. This was very misleading. For example, for Saudi Arabian oil in 1980 the public's cost of production was twenty-nine cents per barrel. The oil sells at the contract price of $24. It sells for more on the spot market. The contract price is eighty-three times the cost, and the difference between the cost and the price is made up by royalties, profits, and taxes. So what are the real costs that the oil companies and the administration said we should pay?

In the United States the price of domestic crude oil was controlled. As of August 1979, the average wellhead price for price-controlled domestic oil was $11.69 per barrel, according to the Department of Energy. Against this, the 1978 average wellhead cost of domestic crude oil, as reported to the Securities and Exchange Commission (SEC) by the seventeen largest oil companies, was only $1.85 per barrel.

The companies complain that SEC accounting methods are unrealistic and that the true costs of production are double this amount. Even if this were true, this would still provide a difference of $7.44 per barrel between cost of production and average wellhead price after correcting for inflation at 15 percent per year. Again, the difference between cost and price is made up by royalties, profits, and taxes. There is no commodity other than crude oil, except possibly electricity, where labor costs are so low and the nonlabor returns are so high in relation to sale price to the consumer.

Impact of Oil Deregulation

Under the oil decontrol program, the average price of controlled oil will rise by more than $12 per barrel at 1980 OPEC prices and 1979 dollars. Decontrol would have little connection with the real costs of production, including workers' wages, but it will certainly increase returns from royalties, profits, and, again, taxes. Decontrol of domestic crude oil will cost the average U.S. family of four more than $500 per year. Even without another OPEC price increase, decontrol of domestic crude would mean the average price of all products would go up another ten cents per gallon at least.

Arguments offered for decontrol of domestic oil by oil companies and the administration were twofold. The first argument was that high oil prices would produce conservation. This is *rationing by price*: raising prices so that poorer consumers cannot afford to buy, while the wealthy are scarcely affected. Rough calculations can be made of the monetary cost per barrel of oil conserved by the rationing-by-price method. Oil product prices nearly doubled from 1979 to 1980. Average consumption was down 5 percent, a reduction of 343 million barrels annually. This kind of conservation is costing consumers nearly $400 per barrel of oil conserved by the rationing-by-price method. Costs in human misery during the winter because of high heating oil prices cannot be calculated.

The second argument used by the oil companies and the administration for higher oil prices was that higher prices would bring about more oil drilling and oil production in this country. Domestic oil production would reduce U.S. dependence on certain foreign sources of supply. This objective perhaps might be desirable if it worked. Present facts, however, do not support the idea that higher oil prices would bring forth substantial addition to domestic production. The average price of controlled domestic oil increased by 50 percent between 1979 and 1980, but U.S. oil production declined by 2 percent.

The oil industry and the Department of Energy have prepared various estimates of the amount of additional oil production they say might be brought about by complete oil decontrol. Full crude oil decontrol would mean that crude oil prices would rise by 100 percent, but what would that do for us?

Decontrol cannot be the basis of any effective national energy plan. Rationing by price places an enormous burden on consumers for trivial gains in oil conservation. Any additional production comes at a very high cost per annual barrel.

The Union's Solution

The Oil, Chemical and Atomic Workers Union starts with the unquestionable proposition that companies are in the business to make money. Accordingly, if more money is to be made by Mobil, Exxon, and the rest of the multinational oil companies by importing oil, instead of producing it in this country, they will import. In short, the profits to be made, not the prices, determine the choice, by these companies, between importing and producing here.

There are a number of reasons why importing crude oil into the United States is more profitable than producing it here. We need to look carefully at these reasons because they provide the key to an energy plan that really would reduce oil imports. The first reason for the higher profitability of oil imports is that income taxes on foreign operations are dollar-for-dollar deductible against U.S. federal income taxes as foreign income tax credits. State income tax paid on domestic productions are counted as ordinary business deductions worth only about 50 percent of the state tax paid on the federal income tax. The Internal Revenue Service has no state income tax credits. You do not have to be a certified accountant to see that foreign income tax credits account for the extraordinarily small income tax paid by the multinational oil companies compared to corporations that are purely domestic. You can also see how foreign income tax credit might make it more profitable to import foreign oil instead of producing domestic oil. As a first step toward taking the profits out of foreign imports, the federal government should eliminate all foreign tax credits not required by existing tax treaties.

A second reason for higher profitability to the multinationals for importing instead of producing domestically is entitlement benefits on imported oil. In November 1979, this benefit was $4.30 per barrel—it totaled almost $10 billion per year in subsidy, facilitating the import of foreign oil. The money comes from the domestic oil producers through Department of Energy entitlements programs.

Recent balance sheets of the domestic producers show they can well afford to pay the entitlements fee; however, it is easy to see that entitlements for the multinational oil companies provide a powerful incentive for the import of oil instead of increasing production from their domestic oil properties. Put yourself in the position of the president of an oil company. In importing, you get $4.30. In producing here, you pay $4.30. Which would you do?

Here is a way to help take the profits out of importing foreign oil: retain 1980 prices of crude oil to the refineries. Let the multinationals pay the entitlements benefits on imported oil without permitting pass-throughs to the consumers. This is a basic program for reducing oil imports.

Note

1. U.S., Congress, House, Subcommittee on Commerce, *Congressional Record*, 96th Cong., 1980, p. E1117.

Questions and Answers to Part II

Question: Mr. Moore, did I hear correctly that the retail price of gasoline has gone up a lot more than the price of OPEC oil? The numbers I have indicate that the price of gasoline has not gone up at the same rate as the price of a barrel of crude of OPEC, and I wonder if you would elaborate on your basis for saying the opposite.

Answer: The price increase from 1972 to today would represent roughly a seven-year span of time, and in that span of time, you are correct, the crude oil prices increased faster. But we have to look at gasoline prices over the last two years. The comparison I wish to make is that prices have increased substantially and are increasing substantially, at the rate of two cents per gallon per week. It is conceivable that, based on the 1979 average price per gallon at seventy cents—and now in 1980 we are looking at almost double that price—that is the correlation we have to make with regard to the prices.

Question: Mr. Moore, would you comment as to what position your union has taken on declining productivity in the labor force in the United States, and what you are doing about it.

Answer: Management determines the level of productivity. An employee or a member of my union has little or nothing to do with productivity. Management sets the policies; they set the levels by which they wish to get out production and that determines productivity. Productivity of the refineries is down from the previous year; again, this was a management prerogative. We are often accused of being lazy workers and of not putting out as much as we used to in the good old days, but the basic premise has to be that an employee does only what he is advised or instructed to do and failing to do that, management has the right to apply disciplinary measures accordingly.

Question: Mr. Moore, have you analyzed the impact of decontrol of domestic crude oil on members of your union?

Answer: Decontrol would not have an impact one way or the other on members of the union. They are paid for their labor. Often we are accused of biting the hand that feeds us, and I certainly do not wish to project that image. Oil company policies are determined by federal bureaucracy; the deregulation is determined by the Congress; the administration is involved in this. We are basically a consumer-oriented union, and we recognize that

if decontrol can work in the petroleum industry as it did in the airline industry, this will be a benefit to the people we represent. And whereas our
members may be 200 thousand, in terms of families we represent some half
a million people, and this is where we are concerned. Deregulation has no
effect whatsoever on the membership.

Question: But deregulation hurts refineries. Mrs. Wilson pointed out that it
is very important for leading technological nations to contribute their share
to Third World development. A great deal of the assistance we could provide is through buying their products. In many Third World nations that
product is oil. Now, with deregulation, essentially—exclusively—domestic
oil would be refined. If you do that, (1) you cut down the cash flow to Third
World nations, and (2) the unions of the maritime industry would have a
great deal to say if this "pipeline" were cut off. Oil does not jump instantaneously from foreign wellheads to United States' refineries. Could you
comment?

Answer: First, the maritime organization is not the exclusive representative
body of those carriers. It represents, on the contrary, less than 10 percent.
    Second, I agree we do have an obligation to those developing countries
to establish trade policies. However, we have gone beyond the simple principle of fair trade. We have become hostage to a complicated situation
where U.S. multinational oil companies have, through arrangement with
OPEC countries, developed a relationship whereby we are now practically
at war over the importation of oil.
    Third, I happen not to believe that we are in such a critical situation that
oil policies should have an impact on our social lives to the extent that low-
and middle-income Americans are unable to pay for heating. I do not
believe the condition is quite so bad that we have become hostage to foreign
countries for fuel.

Answer: (John Naisbitt) Mrs. Wilson very eloquently put this problem in
the real context, the global context. Marshall McLuhan the other day said
there are no passengers on Spaceship Earth. We're all crew! I think we are
getting more of a sense of that. We are becoming more and more a global
village because of jet airplanes and communications satellites.
    Within all of this there is a profound resorting of who is going to make
what in this world. There is an international redivision of labor going on.
Bailing out Chrysler is turning the automobile industry into an employment
program, the way the British turned steel into an employment program.
Now, if we cannot see any farther down the line than that, we are not going
to solve any of these problems. The mature industries in the developed
countries—steel, appliances, automobiles—are going to be imitated by

others. There are eighty-six countries in the world today with automobile assembly plants, and we have no manifest destiny over production.

We have got to concentrate. There are four great areas of technological adventure in this world today. One is electronics with microprocessors; another is the bioindustry with its recombinant DNA—and biology is going to be to the twenty-first century what chemistry and physics were to this century. Alternative sources of energy is the third great technological adventure, whether we find anything or not; and the last is resources from the ocean, mining the seabeds. We have got to look at how we are going to deal with energy and our other problems; look at them ecologically, look at them holistically, and look at them in the context of change and not be rooted to the old world.

Question: Mr. Naisbitt, you had a phrase that was particularly clever: How would we learn from the future? It sounds like a profitable skill.

Answer: We have to structure the future as best we can and then calibrate what we do toward it. And my example of the world resorting itself, who is going to make what, is what the future is all about. If we can anticipate the new shapes, then in connection with our economic policies and our energy policies and so forth, we can learn from the future. We can learn from what is going to happen and that can instruct us as to what we should do today.

Question: Mr. Naisbitt, could you comment on what you think the future looks like for the centralization of energy? For example, will it be synfuels, shale oil, clustering of nuclear power plants? On the other hand, there are advocates of decentralized energy: photovoltaic cells on rooftops, wind machines, and biomass supplements.

Answer: Any kind of centralization is going to have a very hard time in this environment. It is really out of tune with the times. Even something like gasoline rationing, a centralizing phenomenon, is so unpalatable that what finally passed in the Congress was really laughable because it did not allow the president to do anything unless Congress came back to say it was okay. With energy solutions it is going to be very difficult in this environment to employ centralized mechanisms. The direction is clearly decentralized—but not either/or.

It might be appropriate for some of the things we do to be centralized. It is in a multiple option context; not one or the other. We are moving more and more toward emphasis on diversity of fuel sources but that mix is going to differ geographically. If you are in Pennsylvania, and you have unemployment and you are sitting on top of coal, coal is going to be more of your mix.

Even in corporate organizations, I always got the feeling that the important thing was not that you used centralizing or decentralizing labels but that you were doing one or the other. It was the process that got everyone's attention. Our large institutions, because the problems of participation are a question of scale, are going to break down and be restructured as confederations of entrepreneurs within even the largest companies.

Question: Mrs. Wilson, there seems to be a basic conflict when it comes to the costs of new energy policy development and giving appropriate consideration to the impacts that energy policy may have on certain sectors of our population. Should energy policy be developed independently of the potential adverse costs on certain elements of our society or should those adverse impacts be simultaneously addressed by the government or by other policymaking mechanisms?

Answer: I am inclined to agree with the latter. We have to be realistic about where we are with respect to this whole energy matter. I get the impression that we have been subsidizing the cost of energy in this country for many many years. Now we are in the midst of reaping the burden of all of it; we are going to have to develop a strategy that gets us out. I do not think energy prices are going down, they are going up. It would be a catastrophe if we reached the point where we wake up one morning to find that the supply of what makes this country tick is suddenly being pulled out from under us. That kind of havoc will affect everybody in America, the rich as well as the poor folks. I am concerned about addressing this issue responsibly, exploring alternate sources as promptly and as carefully as we can, and insisting that we build a support system that will make it possible to keep unusual hardships from happening.

Answer: (L. Calvin Moore) I am certainly not in disagreement with what you say. I had the opportunity to attend the seminar at which the NAACP policy statement was established. I am in full accord that the NAACP has an obligation to look at any program that will basically create more jobs for minority people.

I am not in agreement that energy development will inherently bring about more employment of minority people. I am convinced, having worked in the energy union for all these years, that that is not the case. From the early 1930s to the present date there is a small ratio of minority workers in the oil industry. It is absent in the nuclear area, in our shale development and tar sands, and in all of the other exotic energy matters that we are attempting to develop.

But the thrust of my statements was directed at the oil companies. Because of the policies developed by the government as a result of the lobbying efforts of the oil industry, we have a situation that has brought about tremendous strain and hardship on poor and middle-class people.

Question: Mrs. Wilson, would you tell us about NAACP activities in areas of developing nations where blacks would be very effective?

Answer: We are just starting, and we are doing it through an International Affairs Committee that we hope to have staffed very shortly. The NAACP is not new to international relations, but we are new in terms of its economic aspects. We hope to have an exciting interchange between our association and this whole field, which we think is crucial to the solution of some of our long-term problems.

Question: Mrs. Wilson and Mr. Naisbitt, in view of the social decentralism that seems to be occurring with the multiple options, do you also see decentralization in the technological field, particularly with respect to ocean energy systems such as OTEC (Ocean Thermal Energy Conversion), which requires an enormous technological and capital investment to produce economically viable energy sources?

Answer: (John Naisbitt) Yes. This clearly engages notions of appropriate scale. Appropriate scale is an interesting phenomenon that goes back to Schumacher's alternative intermediate technology. The appropriate scale for putting gasoline in an automobile is the neighborhood service station —a marvelous example of appropriate scale. The appropriate scale of oil exploration is huge. In government, the appropriate scale for raising an army is like exploration, it is national, it is huge. The appropriate scale for welfare, in my own view, may well be a neighborhood where everybody knows everybody. We are looking at the appropriateness of a lot of things. Again, it is not either/or. It is another multiple option.

Question: Mr. Naisbitt, you said that 55 percent of our work force is engaged in information—that has some tremendous implications. Could you identify who makes up that population? What percent of our GNP is contributed by that group? If it is significantly less, what implications are there for the future? Are oil and energy and the marketplace and society really the key, or is it the change of society itself? I ask this question at the risk of identifying myself as an oil executive.

Answer: The oil companies are in a very interesting place. If they stay in the business they are in, they are going out of business, right? We just do not know how long it is going to take. In the meantime, you are piling up cash, and your dilemma is what to use that money for—to buy or to diversify. You have the problem of purchasing the future. Really an interesting question.

Going back to your question, information occupations are those involved in creating, processing, or distributing information. It is all the news, publishing, and so forth; it is education, it is certainly government— although as far as I can tell, they only write memos. It is certainly everyone in banks—they do not even see the money, they just process the information. The stock market processes information. What we do occupationally structures the society, just as it did when we were all farmers. Now, many more than half of us spend our days processing information, and that fact helps to structure the society. It is very difficult for people to get a handle on information as a world commodity. We keep thinking of the people who process information as overhead—that it is the steel or the oil that makes the money.

Information makes money as well; we are selling information all the time. One quick example: I am on the Board of Directors of CRS, a conglomerate of architectural and engineering firms which also goes back to resorting in this global village. We just got a $100 million contract to build three hotels in the Middle East. The hotel room modules, right down to the soap dishes, are being fabricated in Brazil. Labor is coming from South Korea, and we Americans are providing the construction management, the information function. That is a model. But we have got to think about information as a world commodity because that is the direction we are going. Americans are going to provide that management and the information side.

Part III
Economic Consequences of Energy Policies

Introduction to Part III

Francis X. Murray

One of the problems we face today, as individuals, businesses, and governments, is the fact that the ground rules regarding energy, its use, and its role in our society and our economy have shifted very dramatically in the last few years. It causes us to reflect on and review the appropriateness and the prudence of past energy policies and the difficulties to which they have led us, both in the recent past and today. But we have to accept the realities that energy is more scarce and more expensive, that the price to use includes not only the economic terms but often political conditions that accompany it, and that the situation will likely continue.

As a matter of national pride, we often point to our ability to adapt and change to new situations and new challenges. In the energy area we have found this very difficult. We know from nature that if an organism does not adapt and change, it does not survive. This carries a very uneasy message for our energy policy—one that does not leave us feeling particularly comfortable. Adaptation is not without its problems, pain, and dislocations.

Adaptation often falls unevenly on various segments of society. As a result, the adjustment process has become highly emotional at times. It is wrought with political pitfalls and social difficulties as we strive—in addition to solving our energy problems—to maintain some equity or fairness about how the solutions will be brought about. And, of course, the faster we attempt to bring this change about, the more severe and difficult these pressures are going to become.

As a result, the energy policy with which we find ourselves reflects, at least in part, an effort by political decision makers to defer, or perhaps mitigate, the pain and the symptoms of our energy problem; it reflects the hope that the burdens associated with these changing ground rules will somehow or other, sometime or other, come into play without the hard political decisions that we have been confronted with in the past.

Governments' Roles in Energy Shortage

Jude Wanniski

I was in New Orleans a short time ago at a convention of the Independent Petroleum Association of America, representing about 5,000 wildcat wells. Dr. Michael Halbouty, a world-renowned geophysicist and a wildcatter as well, spoke on the future of liquid petroleum and gas. He made the statement that there are no shortages of energy anywhere on earth that are not caused by governments. And the thing that thrilled me about this, because I am not really an energy wildcatter myself, is that there was a standing ovation. All 2,000 independent petroleum wildcatters recognized the truth of that statement and jumped to their feet.

Mineral Rights Are Key

In the last 120 years, 3.2 million oil wells have been drilled in the crust of the planet. And out of that, 2.4 million were drilled in the oil patch of the United States, the Sun Belt states—not even including Alaska.

The reason all those wells were drilled in the United States was not because God put most of the oil there. It is because economic conditions in the United States throughout the last 120 years were superior to those anywhere else in the world. Out of all those 3.2 million wells drilled, 96 percent were located in the United States, in Western Europe, and in the Soviet Union. Only 4 percent were drilled in Asia, the subcontinent, Africa, Latin America, South America, Australia, New Zealand, and so forth.

The Middle East has not yet been explored. In the last five years in the entire Middle East only an average of seventy-five exploration wells have been drilled per year. In Iraq, in the last five years, there have been only five exploration wells drilled—an average of one per year. In Saudi Arabia, seven per year.

What were the conditions in the United States that caused three out of every four oil wells to be drilled here? The answer is that the United States was the land of opportunity at one time, and it could be again. In the United States over the last 200 years, an individual could possess a deed to a patch of land and the mineral rights appended to that deed. He could arrange with an oil man, an oil company, or a wildcatter to explore for oil on that property, and if oil were discovered, both the driller and the owner would know that their government would not confiscate the proceeds of the discovery, that seven-eighths would go to the oil man, and one-eighth would go to the owner. It would not be confiscated either through nationalization of the property or through confiscatory tax rates.

The reason so few wells are drilled in the Third World, or in China, Africa, Latin America, the Middle East, even in Mexico, is that these conditions do not apply. Either individuals cannot possess property themselves—the government will own most of the land, as in Australia, where 90 percent of all three million square miles are owned by the crown—or the mineral rights do not go along with the property. In Mexico, anything under the ground is owned by the government.

In a Third World country, even where oil can be found, for instance, by a major oil company negotiating with the government, almost each oil well has to be negotiated before exploration proceeds. Individuals who are involved in the process of exploration and drilling, right down to the roughnecks, have incomes that are taxed at such high rates it is not economical to do the kind of mass exploration that was conducted in the United States.

So you could say the energy problems of the world could be solved fairly rapidly through land reform. If in Africa or South America, a political movement suddenly gave individuals mineral rights to their property, you would find indigenous oil companies springing up just as they did in the United States after 1859. So land reform could be one solution. But if not land reform, do we then face a Malthusian picture of the world running out of energy in the latter part of this century?

Inflation and Taxes Are the U.S. Problems

Assuming that there will not be any political changes around the world that will result in the kind of land reform that would elicit new sources of liquified petroleum and gas, what limits the United States' ability to trade for world oil? The energy consequences of economic policy: what we have seen unfold in the last dozen years is the collision worldwide (especially in the United States) of inflation and progressivity in tax systems, smothering our ability to produce U.S. goods and services and technology that could be traded for the oil existing elsewhere in the world.

To illustrate this point, in 1974, William Simon, the Secretary of the Treasury, came home from a visit to the OPEC countries during the embargo. He brought back a recommendation that the United States break OPEC through austerity; we tighten our belts, conserve rapidly, increase taxation on domestic consumption of oil, force down the demand for OPEC oil, and therefore force OPEC to lower the price. I was then writing editorials on energy and economics for the *Wall Street Journal*. I went to

Simon and suggested to him that this was a perverse policy, that the solution to OPEC is not U.S. austerity, but U.S. expansion—economic expansion.

The problem, I said, is that you are looking at OPEC as if we are demanders of energy and they are suppliers of it, and you are not looking at the trading relationship. They are demanders of goods that we produce and we are suppliers of goods in exchange. In other words, they are not selling oil for money. They are trading oil for goods and services. Those goods and services are broken down into current goods and future goods. In other words, we will get a barrel of oil from them; they may get a consumer good and a capital good that they can use immediately, or they can get a future good, a financial asset, a bond that they can cash in thirty years from now. And they are interested in trading for both of these kinds of commodities.

If you cause austerity or recession in the United States as a way of breaking OPEC, I argued to Simon, you would cause a decline in the value of U.S. financial assets. The OPEC countries would quickly lose their appetite for one of the things they are interested in trading with us; that is, financial assets. Or, take those countries, like Venezuela or Iran, which are using all their oil to buy either consumer goods or capital goods—taking the path of industrialization. Venezuela is building capital goods, infrastructure, manufacturing capacity for the oil they are sending us. If the United States' economy goes into recession, then they will slow down their importation of capital goods.

If you had an expansion of the U.S. economy you would increase the value of U.S. financial assets more rapidly than the appreciation of oil in the ground. You would also increase the appetites of oil-producing nations in ways to suggest that it would be in their interest to trade more oil. The competition would then be on their side for our goods and services. The price, the real price, of oil would fall as it was produced in greater quantities.

Looking back at the projections of Aramco (Arabian American Oil Company) and Saudi Arabia in 1970 (before all of these problems occurred in the U.S. economy through inflation and progressivity in tax systems) it is evident that they were, at that time, calculating that by 1980 Saudi Arabian production could increase to 18 million barrels a day. Instead in 1980 they are lifting 9.5 million barrels a day; Saudi Arabia is certainly not getting its money's worth because the financial assets it acquires from us are melting away.

Dollar-denominated financial assets are a problem that afflicts Saudi Arabians, Kuwaitians, and all the OPEC countries with regard to their desire to trade oil to us for our goods, but it is also a problem that affects the Toledo carpenter and the Kansas City dentist. Everyone in the world who now sells for dollars is in a sense being cheated by our government, which is flooding the world with paper dollars. This is the reason the savings rate in the United States has now dropped to a historic low, why productivity in the United States is now in negative numbers. It is not that the American people have lost their sense of thriftiness, but there is no longer an instrument by which they can save. Any dollar-denominated financial assets you could store, your wealth will erode as rapidly if you are in Toledo as it will if you are in Saudi Arabia.

Solution Is Stable, After-Tax Real Dollars

The solutions to these energy problems lie in the direction of internal reforms in the United States that could spread worldwide. One reform is a return to a dollar tied to something of value—a return to a monetary standard that assures the oil-producing nations of the world (as well as individuals) that a dollar asset will be worth the same thirty years from now as it is today. That is the first reform, and it will require at some point reopening the gold window that President Nixon closed on 15 August 1971, bringing us the problems that we have in energy today.

Another reform will deal with the fact that inflation has increased the tax rates, not only in the United States, but everywhere in the world hit by inflation. Except for a few countries, there is progressivity in tax systems everywhere, demanding a tax reform in the United States that brings real rates of taxation on personal incomes back to about 1970 levels.

An extreme situation exists in Turkey, our NATO ally of 50 million people. We are now in the process of losing Turkey as we have lost Afghanistan into the Soviet orbit, and lost our influence in Iran. For Turkey it is part, again, of the foreign-policy consequences of economics. At least eight devaluations have occurred in Turkey over the last ten years, induced by the International Monetary Fund (IMF) representing western bankers who want to get paid back the money the Turks borrowed from us earlier. After the recession hit in 1974, the Turks needed money. They came to the IMF's western banks, who said, "Okay, we'll lend you some more money, but you will have to undergo a devaluation; you'll have to proclaim an austerity policy, you'll have to increase taxes."

What has happened in Turkey is that the progressive tax system has been left unchanged since 1970. The whole private sector of the Turkish economy has been wiped out. The only commerce transacted is either through the government or black market. To stave off financial crisis in January 1980, the Turkish government received another $600 million to service the $15 billion debt it owes to the western bankers. No resources come into Turkey, just more borrowing to finance more debt—in exchange for an agreement wrung out of Turkey by the IMF for another 48 percent devaluation of the Turkish lira.

You can see the global problem of the impact of inflation and progressivity up the Laffer curve. Inflation and tax rates not only squeeze out the ability of people to produce shoes, farm produce, and even widgets, but energy as well. The solutions to the world's energy problems lie in the kinds of reforms described here. There are no energy problems that exist anywhere in the world that are not caused by governments.

7 Effect of Energy Policies on Oil Supplies

David Sternlight

With regard to energy, we seem to have good news now—decontrol and a situation in which we are going to institute progressive policies about energy. In reality what we have is a variety of tax elements that suppress supply of conventional oil and gas.

The policies being put together by Congress on the tax side are somewhat counterproductive to supply, in the face of what now appears to be an outlook for a significant lowering of U.S. oil and gas production over the next five to ten years. At a time when we should be looking at incentives to increase supply, we are putting in various elements that represent political compromises of one sort or another that will act in the opposite direction.

Another factor in the same set of policies is the translation of what was expected to be, and what was announced to be, a windfall profits tax. It is not really a windfall profits tax, it is an excise tax; that is, you pay the tax as a function of the difference between the price you get and some stated prices regardless of your profits. What should have been a windfall profits tax bill, to compensate for the much higher revenues that oil companies would receive, is instead becoming a revenue bill. If you look at some of the spending commitments being made right now by Congress for that bill's revenues, you will see they are not keying it to the sort of things that are energy related but to a number of other expenditures. These revenues, once built into the system, will have such enormous political attractiveness it is unlikely that the government will ever want to let go of them. So we see the windfall profits tax becoming a kind of a permanent revenue bill. That is another element of policy that seems to be counterproductive to the supply of conventional oil and gas.

There are a variety of overt and subtle subsidies built into the system that are suppressing alternatives—geothermal, other forms of energy, including the rapid development of the renewables we must have if we are going to make the transition from exhaustible oil and gas to more benign, more environmentally sound, more attractive forms of energy supply. Built into the system are a variety of market obstacles which suppress decentralized energy sources. Electric utilities, for example, cannot compete in cogeneration and other decentralized markets. The incentives are not there. The result is that some electric utilities are still resisting some of those forms of energy efficiency and improved conservation because they see those as markets in which they cannot participate but which threaten their business base.

Economic Insanity

Economic insanity exists in some proposals for getting us out of this dilemma. I think in particular of the orginal presidential proposal for synthetic fuels, which essentially said there is a national security case to be made for a certain volume of energy at above-OPEC prices. After some analysis of varying kinds, the argument was that perhaps two million barrels a day was a reasonable volume of incremental supply, or incremental conservation, that could be justified at above-OPEC prices in the national security interest.

And so what follows: a proposal for a production program of synthetics. That reflects, perhaps, the second most expensive alternative you could think of if you were trying to find alternatives a little more costly than OPEC prices. A rational strategy for providing an increment of energy, for example, two million barrels a day, at above-OPEC prices is to look around and say, "What is the cheapest thing that is just more costly than OPEC and how much could we get of that?" And the answer, of course, is conservation.

Can we get two million barrels a day through conservation before we get to a higher price that will trigger something else? If the answer is yes, you put the whole program onto conservation. If the answer is no, you say: "What is the next most expensive source of energy that we could use that is justified above OPEC prices to contribute to the two million barrels a day?" If you still have not got your two million you do the next thing and the next thing.

Finally, if you have not got the full two million and you have reached the trigger price for synthetic fuels, then maybe you want to do some synthetic fuel production, but not before. But that is not the program that is proposed. The program that was originally proposed, and Congress in its wisdom this time saw through that, was to go straight for synthetic production. What we are seeing now is more of a movement toward research, development, and demonstration for synthetics to try to get the price down. That is a little more sensible.

Conservation—this is part of the good news—is stimulated by the higher prices if, in fact, they are allowed to operate through decontrol as the political process unwinds. Make no mistake about this: real price, net of inflation, does influence energy consumption. For quite a long time we saw the use of gasoline increasing, and everyone said, "Oh my gosh, the gasoline price is going up, people are using more; obviously price doesn't affect it."

It turns out that if you take a look at the real price, net of inflation, except for a bubble after the initial Arab embargo, the real price of gasoline in this country has been falling; so naturally people used more. As recently as February of 1979, the real price of average regular gasoline at the pump in the United States was a couple of cents a gallon below the price in August of 1967. Since February, the real price of gasoline, net of inflation, has been rising; since February, suddenly people are using less gasoline. Estimates vary: perhaps 7 percent less is being used, net of economic growth effects, and so on. So once the real price of gasoline started to rise, people did start to behave the way economic theory teaches; people are using less.

The Bad News

The bad news is that interferences with the market are still prevalent in thinking and planning. The notion of import quotas is mentioned, and then people talk in Washington about an escape hatch if this conglomeration of inappropriate policies does not work. The escape hatch is allocation and rationing, and that, especially if it involves a physical denial of energy supplies rather than higher prices for the energy supplies, will, of course, be dislocating to the economy.

The environmental process in this country is still unresolved. We need to make some firm determinations about what would be permitted and what would be prohibited, and then get on with the job. What we actually still see instead is a lot of "ad hoc-ery." The most recent example is the 1979 Alaskan Beaufort Sea lease-sale in which some environmentalists went to court and challenged that lease-sale on grounds that the environmental impact statement was incomplete. The court ruled in their favor and suggested that further judicial review is required. Now it is up to the Interior Department to appeal and try to produce an acceptable environmental impact statement.

Even our emergency provisions are not being followed in an appropriate way. The emergency petroleum stockpile has not been built up for some time. At least they finally got the pumps installed, and we can now get at what we have under the ground. But what we have in the ground in our emergency petroleum stockpile is about a million barrels a day for ninety days. If we face any sort of a significant interruption that cannot be handled by the world oil market and the International Energy Agency sharing plan in some combination, we do not have much of an insurance policy in the emergency petroleum stockpile. In addition, stockpile costs are now skyrocketing. The original $7 billion estimate is now officially $25 billion—unofficially $30 billion—much of that from higher oil costs.

There are apparent difficulties in the western alliance toward cooperation on energy policies. The possibility exists that if import quotas in fact become policy, some significantly destabilizing effects on the economy will be experienced within the next few years. One set of calculations, based on some fairly pessimistic assumptions about real economic growth and on some fairly high OPEC oil-price increases, suggests that by 1984 or 1985 we will be about one and a half million barrels a day above the present import target for the United States. No prizes for guessing what that will do to the economy, if in fact that policy is adhered to, and there is physical rationing and allocation in order to hold to the policy.

Putting all of this together, there is very high uncertainty in the energy outlook. We see ourselves following policies which, while better than the policies of a few years ago, still represent a somewhat incoherent, in many areas counterproductive, set of energy policies. They are counterproductive insofar as suppression of demand and stimulation of supply of both transition fuels and renewable fuels is concerned. I am afraid the economic consequences of all this indicate a period of great difficulty in the 1980s together with a building of social tensions as various interest groups continue in the face of these difficulties to try to secure their level of entitlements that have accumulated with the expectations of the 1960s and 1970s. I am afraid these expectations cannot be fulfilled at historic levels under these and related economic conditions of the 1980s.

8 The Economic Consequences

Andrew Safir

The economic consequences of what is commonly called energy policy are quite apparent: a rapidly rising inflation rate; a very weak dollar in world markets by historical standards; and sluggish U.S. growth rates well below past potentials.

The reason: in reality we do not have an energy policy at all. We have a rather haphazard combination of tax policies, economic policies, diplomatic maneuvers, and social programs that we call an energy policy. None of these approaches deals with the central problem. Put very simply: we are overly dependent on import oil—something we have little control over in terms of price. The central difficulty is that we have no security with foreign supplies.

We are more dependent now on imported oil than in 1973, and present energy policies fail to deal directly with this problem. As a result, what we now have is an economy extremely sensitive to international oil flows—much more sensitive than it was even in 1973. That is particularly important because price changes are not fundamentally destabilizing to the U.S. economy. A run-up in oil prices can be handled. We have handled it before; we are in the process of handling it now.

What really throws us on the ropes in terms of economic growth is oil supply disruption. That will create fundamental problems in an economy that is overly dependent on imported oil. We had a taste of that in the second quarter of 1979 when we had a very short intermittent gas problem in the United States, especially in California. Growth rates in the second quarter were negative. That is the only time they were negative, and it is the only time economists even came close to predicting or finding the recession they were looking for in 1979. This disruption in world oil supplies is the real economic consequence of present energy policies, making us more vulnerable all the time to a situation over which we have very little control.

A few policy alternatives are discussed here. The solution to foreign oil reliance is to reduce our dependence. That seems fairly self-evident. There are three ways we can do this: produce more, find acceptable substitutes for imported oil, and consume less.

Gasoline Taxes

The United States at the moment has the lowest gasoline tax of any industrialized country in the world. I do not think there is any question that increasing it sharply would reduce the demand for gasoline. The 1980 federal tax on gasoline is four cents a gallon in the United States. Combined state and federal taxes on gasoline are fourteen cents. When I last checked, the 1979 average tax in Germany was $1.14; in France, $1.59; in Italy, $1.58—that is for regular gas; the tax goes up for premium.

Unfortunately, higher gas taxes are probably a political impossibility in the United States. Polls show sharp disapproval for increasing gas taxes. Moreover, to the north of us we have a graphic example of what happens to a government that fully intended to increase gasoline taxes. The Clark administration in Canada had, as a major piece of its economic program, an eighteen cents a gallon tax on gasoline. They went down to resounding defeat primarily on that issue. It was an east/west split—producers versus consumers in Canada. Those lessons are not lost on U.S. politicians. We do not have a prayer of getting, even if some of us wanted it, a higher tax on gasoline to a level that would make a difference.

Rationing

We should seriously consider rationing gasoline for our own good. Obviously, there are administrative complexities involved in a rationing scheme. Economists like to assume those things away. I am not going to get bogged down talking about black markets, yellow markets, white markets, and the dirty gray areas in between, and how rationing schemes step on some folks and help others. There are people out there who welcome that sort of analysis; they are called bureaucrats.

Consider the benefits of a rationing program in gasoline. First, we could reduce our dependence on imported oil—the cause of our instability. If we rationed the private automobile sector, we could reduce imported oil without dramatically affecting U.S. rates of growth, an important consideration. We could also improve our balance of payments—no matter the price of oil, within wild limits in any case. We would undoubtedly reduce the erosion of the dollar and probably reduce inflation in the United States as well. Now, strangely enough, rationing is not terribly unpopular in the United States. Polls on rationing in California in 1979 were substantially positive. A San Francisco *Chronicle* poll taken at the end of the gasoline shortage favored rationing by a substantial margin over other forms of energy allocation, including higher taxes or decontrol.

We can make it more popular still by cutting gasoline prices. Decontrol, if we allow it, will probably result in a gas price increase of anywhere from ten to fifteen cents a gallon. If we eliminate state and federal excise taxes on gasoline and ration at the same time, we would limit our imports to a reasonable level and cut the price of gasoline to moderate users. Non-moderate users would probably have the opportunity of purchasing ration tickets in a white market from those who wanted to sell them.

We have about $12 billion in the Highway Trust Fund that we are not using; we do not need to subsidize highway construction any further. I think further subsidy is probably poor federal policy. If you are worried about maintenance, most agencies can maintain highways out of general revenue funds, and they can apply for appropriations as in any other area of government.

From my point of view, there is no energy problem per se. I do see an imported oil problem. I see some straightforward ways of handling it that the federal government has seen fit to ignore: (1) decontrol oil prices rapidly, and impose a rational windfall profits tax to pick up the difference for social reasons; (2) explore a rational substitution policy with strong emphasis on regional uses and not worry about imposing a nuclear policy across the United States—or a coal policy, or a gas policy, or for that matter, a domestic energy policy; and (3) cut consumption through a rationing mechanism and perhaps effect a reduction in the price of gasoline to sweeten the pot.

Without these factors, we are going down the road of increasing dependence on foreign crude. Price will increase. The economy will experience price increases as we increasingly transfer money to OPEC nations. As we transfer money out, our rate of growth will probably decline continuously. We will have a sluggish period of economic growth well into the 1980s and will be more and more on the knife edge, worried about the cutoff. To me that is an unacceptable policy for the federal government to pursue.

Questions and
Answers to Part III

Question: Mr. Wanniski, you mentioned that you thought the dollar should be tied to something stable. Given recent 200 percent increases in the gold price, does gold qualify as being stable?

Answer: Gold is, and has, for millennia, been the most stable of all monetary assets, and what you see now is not the instability of gold. You see the instability of the dollar—wild fluctuations in the marketplace, people betting on the present and future value of the U.S. dollar relative to gold. Since the gold window was closed in 1971, the price of gold in dollars has gone up by a factor of twenty and the price of oil has gone up by a factor of twenty.

When you think of the price of gold going up now to $650 or $700 an ounce, the first thing that follows are the nonrenewable resources. Oil will follow in the world markets, then copper and silver. The last thing to catch up is the price of labor, and that might take five or ten years.

If the monetary authority of the United States were to open the gold window—we now have $200 billion of it in Fort Knox—and announce that six months from now the government will buy and sell gold at whatever the price is that day, then the price of the dollar and the exchange rate of the dollar and gold would be kept constant.

This is the way we ran monetary policy in this country for two centuries, and there was no inflation for two centuries. The use of a monetary standard like gold gives confidence not only in the dollar but in dollar-denominated assets, and people would be willing once again to trade oil, coffee, bananas, anything in greater quantity, in order to acquire dollar-denominated assets.

Question: If I could add a second part to my question, I would also like each of your views on what would happen if OPEC denominates oil in terms of other currencies. What would that do to the Eurodollar market and interest rates?

Answer: (David Sternlight) It depends on the form of it. If OPEC denominates oil in a basket of currencies, but they are willing to take the dollar equivalent of that basket of currencies, then it should not really make much difference. If OPEC insists on physical payment in those currencies, that would abruptly reduce the demand for dollars and abruptly increase the demand for other currencies, the value of the dollar would drop like a shot, and the value of other currencies would increase.

Answer: (Andrew Safir) It really does not matter what OPEC is paid, only what currencies they want to hold. The value of the dollar would remain rock solid if the OPEC countries only wanted to hold dollar reserve assets no matter what currency they were paid in.

When you take a look at the payment side, you are really looking at a simple numeraire. If they choose to diversify rapidly away from the dollar as a reserve asset, then you are going to see a rapid decline in the value of the dollar. If they choose to diversify slowly, you will see a slow erosion, perhaps in dollar values, but even that is not a necessity.

What is worrying most people in the international monetary field at the moment is the sheer amount of liquidity that is available—a sharp departure from dollar-denominated assets that will cause tremendous difficulties for the value of the dollar. One proposed solution is that the International Monetary Fund set up a substitution account that would take dollar assets of IMF members, and issue instead some sort of special drawing right or reserve asset that is a little less volatile than the dollar. We could also insure that the value of the dollars the fund now holds will stay constant. We have not agreed to insure the fund at the moment, but the sizable liquidity is a variable when you talk about using the numeraire and having it float through onto the asset side. And to my mind, what currency you value it in does not mean much: it is what OPEC countries hold and the liquidity—the dollar standing in terms of its liquidity—in world markets at the time they decide to shift their holdings.

Answer: (Jude Wanniski) I agree with very little of that. It comes out of the same framework that led to the breakup of the international monetary system in the first place. There is no dollar overhang. One of the biggest hoaxes the economics profession has foisted on policymakers is that this Eurodollar overhang is about to break off at any minute and engulf us all. This has been a popular idea with the Trilateral Commission, and with the United States Treasury—Fred Bergsten, assistant secretary, has been pushing it for years. Eurodollars are dollars that are being created by private institutions, private individuals in the international banking system, or "ink money," if you will. And there is just no possibility that all of a sudden it would break off and $300 billion worth of demands be put on a certain Tuesday afternoon in the U.S. marketplace.

I really do not know, though, what would happen if the OPEC countries decided to use a different numeraire. I do tend to think with Andrew Safir that you would not immediately see any colossal things happen. But it certainly could not be good because it is another step toward destroying the banking system of the United States as a multinational force, just as we seem determined to destroy our oil companies domiciled in the United States as a multinational force.

Question: Mr. Safir, when is your office going to consider altering the environmental standards so that we can refine and get heavy oil here in California?

Answer: My office is not responsible for environmental standards. Those decisions are made in another area that issues permits—in particular, environmental permits for things like Kern County heavy oil production. They are proceeding as fast as they can, given the constituencies they have to deal with, to see that the heavy oil in California can be pumped out and can be refined within fair quality standards.

A lot of people like the air they breathe, and they are very concerned by any diminution of its quality. Pollution controls in the area where most of our refineries are located are few and far between. Their solutions take time. We are doing a better job there than we were a few years ago. I have not been aware in recent months of any tremendous unhappiness with the speed at which Planning and Research and other California agencies are moving toward facilitating the permit process.

Question: (by Congressman Stockman) Mr. Safir, let me say that every single point you made was completely, totally, and unequivocally wrong. You started by saying that high inflation, the declining dollar, negative productivity, low economic growth, and more, in this country are caused by high energy prices. In Japan, they have high growth, high productivity, and they pay even higher energy prices than we do because they import all of their oil and they've suffered a much higher increase.

Answer: Congressman, we will take these one at a time if that is okay. The Japanese have, between 1973 and 1978, paid in U.S. dollars for their energy. The actual cost to Japan in U.S. dollars in 1978 was 20 percent below what it was in 1973 because the value of the Japanese yen was artificially pumped up against the U.S. dollar.

Question: That was when you had yen going 180 for the dollar. Today it is about 240. Most of that decline in the exchange rate you are talking about has been reversed and it is irrelevant.

Answer: No, using Japan is a poor example. In the 1970s with low energy prices, Japan had a huge export-led economy, very low inflation rates, high employment. Now, in the last year, it is reversed and their value of the yen is down against the dollar, the inflation rate in Japan has been accelerated at quite remarkable rates.

It may be true that a variety of ills I have attributed to U.S. energy policy are fairly only partially attributable to it.

Question: I appreciate your advocacy of decontrol, but I do not think you really mean it. You said we ought to decontrol, institute a windfall profits tax, and just not tax the marginal barrel. I do not know how you define marginal barrel. The marginal barrel can come from anywhere, from a field that was drilled in 1920, if as a result of price change its reuse was justified by some new technology. The greatest examples are the oil companies with fields in East Texas. They have been producing for thirty to forty years; they are about running out. It just happens that those same companies own carbon dioxide wells in New Mexico and Colorado. They could connect the carbon dioxide of the old reservoirs with a $50 million pipeline, inject the old fields full of new carbon dioxide injection wells, and get a lot more oil out over the next twenty years. But if you tax that away, you are not getting the marginal barrel. Are you going to define that as marginal?

Answer: No. Secondary and tertiary recovery can be new oil, if you like.

Question: How do you distinguish on a property by property, well by well, cost by cost basis what is a windfall and what is additional production due to the fact that economics have changed and allowed you to invest more in that property? I do not know how you can possibly do it without fifty thousand bureaucrats!

Interjection by Sternlight: You have got them! They are called the Department of Energy and they do nothing now and you have put them in place! We are sitting around doing nothing because we cannot get some definitions.

President Harry Truman did a brilliant thing when the U.S. economy was on the verge of what economists mistakenly thought would be very, very slow growth after World War II. Truman gave instructions to settle conversion terms for selling U.S. government war production plants to companies which can be summarized: "Look," he said, "we've got to get the country moving again—accept their first offer and we'll sue later if we find any really bad guys in there. Make a simple difinition of the thing and then worry about suing later so we can get on with the job."

Question: (by Congressman Stockman) The overdependency thesis is the rationale for everything you energy bureaucrats are doing. If we had made [Safir] the national energy czar in 1974 and given you power to damp down the oil import level from 8 million to 4 million barrels per day, then last March when the Iranian crisis hit and there was a production outage, can you tell me any single thing that would have been different in terms of the price change in the world market, in terms of the fears that caused inventories to accumulate, in terms of their repercussions internally in the United States?

Answer: You can't base policy on what might happen in a wide range of areas. You have to look around and say to yourself, "What is likely to happen? What is my best guess? What is right when I look ahead?"

Question: I would like to hear your best guess. Tell me what would have happened and how the outcome to the Iranian oil cutoff would have been different.

Answer: If I were the energy czar in 1974, I would probably have embarked on a program to decontrol energy prices, and to . . .

Question: I am not asking what you would have done. I am assuming you were successful, and you got the import rate down from 8 million barrels a day to 4 as of March 1979 when the disruption occurred. Why would the outcome have been different and what would have happened—not in this country but around the world—that would have permitted the outcome to be more salutary?

Answer: First of all, the amount of oil you import is obviously tremendously less, so the dependence on foreign sources is tremendously less. Therefore, the impact of that is tremendously less.

Question: There are grade differentials and transportation, but basically domestic oil prices moved in lock step with the world price, isn't that true?

Interjection by Sternlight: OPEC's ability to raise price is not independent of U.S. imports; the two are closely related. OPEC 's ability to raise price is a function of the domestic revenue needs of particular OPEC countries, their supply potential, the amount of capacity in place, and many other factors. If you reduced U.S. imports from 8 to 4 million barrels a day by the time the Iranian disruption occurred, you would have observed considerably different price behavior by OPEC as a much lower rise in price to handle Iranian oil disruption.

Answer: (Andrew Safir) Even assuming that OPEC was successful in limiting its production to a level that kept world markets tight, the amount of internal dissent among OPEC members would have been increased tremendously. If oil producers get a shortfall as with Iran, there is a tremendous amount of pressure to leap into that gap and to make up the difference, because you never worry about your neighbor. He has a lot of excess capacity and he may want to do it ahead of you. So you have a much less stable cartel under those situations and you have much less likelihood of extreme price rises, even when you have a disruption in one particular country. Reducing our imports would have helped tremendously in keeping the U.S. economy on an even keel even with a disruption like Iran and will in the future if we start now. But if we do not start limiting our imports to some reasonable level, we become more vulnerable, even to small disruptions. And the disruptions of the future may not be quite as small as the 1979 Iranian disruption.

Interjection by Wanniski: Walter Lippmann said in 1970 that he was afraid that we were entering a minor dark age in the world. Many of the things Andrew Safir mentioned suggest that he is already operating in that dark age.

What we would do to prevent OPEC from doing terrible things to us ten years from now is to do terrible things to ourselves today. We could solve our energy problem instantly by shooting every fifteenth motorist. I think this illustrates what Margaret Bush Wilson and Rufus McKinney of the NAACP meant a few years ago when they said it is fine for White House aides to talk about saving energy when they are making $50,000 a year.

The net result of all this is that the poorest people have to pay as a result of all this austerity and belt-tightening. Now we do not have to reduce our dependence on imported oil. We can broaden the portfolio by acting internationally in ways that encourage a multiplication in the number of oil producers, encouraging the kind of ideas that may even sound radical with regard to land reform or reasonable rates of taxation in Third World countries. But it might be preferable to having the International Monetary Fund run around pleading with countries to tax themselves to death so they could produce more oil. The more producers there are then the larger is the portfolio a nation has in drawing on energy. This was the secret of the British Commonwealth in the nineteenth century, having a whole multiplicity of countries associated and affiliated through the magnetism of the home country.

The other thing, as I said before, is that you can manipulate and alter the price of imported oil, real price, by offering better goods in your own marketplace, by offering not only higher quality capital goods and production, not only to OPEC countries, but by having the United States produce better goods, high quality goods, to sell to Belgium in case the Saudis want to trade with Belgium—you have three-way relationships instead of always thinking two-way—and having in our own marketplace higher quality financial assets, a higher quality storehouse of value, that would permit countries selling oil, their patrimony, a store of value when their oil runs out. We are flooding the OPEC countries and our own small investors with worthless paper currency, and that is the struggle that is going on.

Answer: (David Sternlight) I find your arguments singularly unpersuasive. In fact, the argument, "What about the poor people?" is one of the things that hung us up in energy policy for many years.

In answer to the question, "What about the poor people?" this country has a variety of well-established, very powerful policy techniques for income maintenance and other transfers. In fact, Congress has already acted to ameliorate for the poor many of the difficulties of higher energy prices. To make energy policy a hostage to incomes instead of dealing with incomes in the area where we have powerful policy tools seems to me to be one of the things that has caused delays and confusion in this country's energy policy.

Answer: (Jude Wanniski) Margaret Bush Wilson was not talking about the NAACP's stake in maintenance of the dole for poor black people. She is talking about the "land of opportunity" being opened to blacks. Now that they have their civil rights, they have a right to buy a ticket on the train, and all of a sudden the train stops running because the forces of darkness say we have to conserve energy. That is what her statement was about. It is not about welfare and the dole and income maintenance.

Question: I see a connection between decentralization and the desirability of regional approach to use of nuclear, coal, gas, and oil. I share that view, but I wonder if you have any suggestions as to how our legislative process in Washington could achieve such a regional policy.

Answer: (Andrew Safir) Well, I think you are probably going one step too far, too fast. We have first to provide the awareness to policymakers that there is a regional strategy to achieve national objectives. I do not see too many policymakers in Washington taking that focus when they look at problems, and that is really the first step to getting rational legislation. First, we have to convince people who are, by nature, central government folks, and when they talk about central government, that means the government of the people for everybody, everybody identical. To get them to think that they have objectives that can be achieved in a variety of ways is another matter.

One of the areas that upsets many economists, for example, is the idea that perhaps unemployment is essentially a regional problem in the United States. There are pockets of unemployment here, there are pockets there, and the typical reaction to a high level of unemployment is to reinflate the economy to try to get rid of it. So you can apply a broad-brush approach to what is essentially a regional problem, and as a result, you do not do well in specific regions and you cause problems for the nation as a whole.

I do not yet see the awareness among public policymakers of the concept of regionality. It is something we in the regions have been trying to explain in Washington for quite a while, and the receptivity is not there yet. So, rather than attempt a strategy to get laws passed through Congress that make some sense in a regional framework, I would settle for pounding a little regional framework thinking into central government thinkers. That would be the first step to getting any law passed in Congress.

Part IV
International Attitudes
toward U.S. Oil Policies

Introduction to Part IV

Yahia Abdul-Rahman

Two of the most significant developments in the oil industry are taking place: one has just occurred in the 1970s, the other is about to occur in the 1980s. The first was the takeover of production rights by the OPEC countries from the oil companies. The second is the takeover of marketing rights by OPEC countries from the major oil companies.

The implication of the second development is far-reaching; it will bring oil producers closer to the marketplace to feel the pulses of the market in a more effective way. For example, the Iranian government recently tested the market by floating a tanker on the spot market. These developments will impact on the production policy of the producing countries.

A large number of international issues needs to be discussed. Consider the following:

1. How does OPEC view the West and how does the West view OPEC? Is it a financial, energy supply-and-demand situation, or is it a cultural situation that we need to examine?
2. The use of the U.S. dollar as a medium of exchange and the resulting implication of monetary and fiscal policies in the United States.
3. The resulting new force of non-OPEC producers and their pricing policies. Mexico, which the United States thought would stabilize prices, is taking the lead in following the OPEC pricing mechanism: The North Sea producers are doing the same, essentially. What about the situation of decontrolling oil prices and the resulting price structure in the United States?
4. How are we to reduce imports into the United States; what about the position of allies, especially Japan, France, and West Germany, competing with the United States in the marketplace but not cooperating to stabilize the market?
5. The uneven pricing of crude oil to oil companies. Many of the "seven sisters" obtain preferential treatment on buying their crude oil, compared to companies that buy oil on the spot market.
6. Government-to-government transactions, and justification of the U.S. government's takeover of the purchase of crude oil.
7. The destabilizing role of crude oil independent traders in the marketplace, and the problems of speculation.
8. The subject of payoffs. A company with ethical values that decides not to pay off is limited in conducting its business and is deprived of a long-

term relationship beneficial to both the people of the producing government and the customers of the buying company.

9. Last, political matters, such as the United States policy regarding illegal
   aliens from Mexico and its impact on Mexican government supply
   policy to the United States, the long-standing Arab-Israeli problem,
   and also the recent Iranian government crisis.

Views of the Oil-Producing Countries

Hussein Abdallah

Egypt is not a major producer of oil. This year we will produce nearly 600,000 barrels per day: one-third to meet domestic needs, one-third exported by our national company, EGPC, and one-third taken by foreign companies as cost recovery and company share under the country's production-sharing agreements.

Egypt is not a member of OPEC, either. We have no direct involvement in OPEC's pricing system and resolutions. We are a member of OAPEC, sometimes referred to as the Arab OPEC, which includes, in addition to seven Arab country members of OPEC, three non-OPEC Arab countries. OAPEC activities have centered on Arab petroleum joint ventures—four of which are already operative with a combined capital of nearly $2 billion. In general, we are intensifying investments to enlarge the resource base in order to provide the world with more oil and help relieve the energy crisis.

However, after spending five years as professor of petroleum economics at Kuwait University, and particularly since my return to Egypt in 1974, I have been deeply involved in the current international dialogue between developing and developed countries. Having spent eighteen months as the representative of my country in the North-South Dialogue at Paris, and having been a participant in international conferences and seminars on the topic, I would like to convey to you some views of the oil-producing countries.

Oil-Producing Countries' Concern with Development

There are two major differences between an oil producer and an oil consumer. The immediate problem of energy in the United States does not go beyond this year—maybe a month; its focus of interest stops at the gasoline lines that might affect the rushing life of the American citizen. This narrow framework reflects a sharp contrast to both the time spectrum and the focus of attention of the oil-producing countries.

All oil producers are developing countries, and oil is still the backbone of their economies and development process. Oil is their only chance to get developed and attain a reasonable standard of living. Since development is a slow process (for instance, in Japan), they have to be concerned not only with today but for fifty years from now and even longer.

Since the governments of the oil-producing countries obtained their sovereign right over this natural wealth only a few years ago, they are still influenced by a long history of bitterness and grievances. In order to understand their actions today, and ultimately cooperate with—instead of confront—them, we should go back in history. Fifty years into the past and another fifty into the future is the producer's time spectrum, as compared with the immediate present for the private consumer. A producer's focus of attention is concerned with the long-range development process, while an oil consumer worries about a gasoline line and a few cents more in the price of energy. With these differences in mind, I will overview parts of history to help describe today's oil market behavior and performance.

OPEC did not design or structure the oil market. OPEC inherited a structure that had been in other hands for more than 50 years and was ready to explode. International oil companies knew this and knew they could still make money while oil is in OPEC hands, as they did when oil was in their own hands. With a rapidly depleting resource, prices would have to go up; with higher prices, the companies may make even more money while the blame goes to OPEC.

Neither the oil companies nor OPEC need always bear the blame. There is not much they can do if the market were restructured in such a way as to provide stability over the long range. In the current circumstances, restructuring may be brought about mainly through the introduction of alternative energy sources and energy conservation. I hope that it will not be too late to recognize that OPEC is in fact rendering a better service to consumers than any other alternative would do—including the elimination of OPEC and setting free all oil producers to serve their own interests.

Oil Producers Powerless in History

As shown by the U.S. case against the international petroleum cartel, a price war erupted in 1927 between the two giants of the oil industry; namely, Standard Oil of New Jersey and Shell Oil Company. This worldwide price war ended with the parties signing a cartel agreement in September 1928.

Many would condemn this agreement as a restrictive monopoly, negatively affecting the consumer. I tend to differ. In certain cases, monopoly may be the most efficient way to run an industry, provided it is subjected to reasonable control by public authorities. In other cases monopoly may be a temporary remedy to save an industry from bankruptcy, and this was the case with the oil industry in the 1930s. In addition, the oil industry was facing a severe glut, further worsened by the discovery of East Texas oil fields that drove the price to a devastating level of ten cents a barrel. Funds needed to explore and develop oil would have been in severe deficiency, and this might have caused fatal damage to the rapidly flourishing automobile and aircraft industries.

On the other hand, the cartelization movement of the 1930s gave rise to a wider company base. The three signing parties (including British Petroleum) became seven or eight, and other major suppliers joined the arrangement by their actions if not by formal signing. Roumanian and Soviet oil, which by then was an important part of the international oil supply, followed the pattern. This was especially clear after the 1932 conference held by the American Petroleum Institute to deal with the problem of oil conservation. Early oil history has ever since been repeating itself, which reflects forces inherent in the industry.

An example is the oil-pricing system, which is mainly governed by the relationship among market structure, behavior, and performance. Prior to World War II, when the United States was the world's major supplier of oil (together with the Caribbean area it provided nearly three-quarters of international oil), it was only logical that oil be priced on the basis of a single point—the Gulf Plus Formula.

When in the 1940s the Middle East emerged as a major supply area, the pricing system had to change to the so-called Dual-Basing Point. Due to certain vested interests, the new formula could not continue to its logical and stable limits. The United States has become a net oil importer since 1948. Western Europe and Japan were experiencing a fast reconstruction process, and coal, though accounting for 85 percent of the latter's energy needs, was not available in the required amounts. On the other hand, the huge Middle Eastern oil fields, which were discovered and shut in before World War II, had to meet the rapidly growing need for energy in the western countries. Thus, the share of Middle Eastern oil in the world oil supply continued to rise from 17 percent in 1938 to 40 percent in 1949, to 51 percent during the 1960s, and to nearly 60 percent during the 1970s.

A sticky and slow response to the new realities of the market structure led to the creation of OPEC in 1960. During that period, the international oil companies had a free hand over the industry by means of the so-called Concession System established during the 1920s and 1930s, when the oil-producing countries were in a state of severe underdevelopment. Western governments interfered, when necessary, in policies that dealt with the international oil industry. Examples: the Red Line Treaty of the 1920s; the pricing of oil products needed for American and British fleets during World War II; the nationalization of oil by Iran in 1951; and the first Suez crisis in 1956, which ended up by establishing permanent machinery within OECD (then OEEC) that became the basis for the establishment of the International Energy Agency (IEA) in 1974.

Under the dual-basing point system, the price of Middle Eastern oil had to be equalized with the price of western hemisphere oil at an imaginary point on a Cif basis. When these two prices were equalized on a FOB (freight on board) basis prior to 1947, this imaginary point was near Malta, giving the Middle East an economic advantage over areas east of the equalization point. To allow Middle Eastern oil to flow west, the oil companies, through a series of complex changes, kept reducing prices of Middle East oil until the equalization point reached London and further moved to New York.

This was a deviation from sound economics, since Western Europe at the time accounted for 55 percent of Middle East oil exports, while the United States accounted for only 8 percent. The equalization point should have remained at London, thus narrowing the gap by which the Middle East price had to be reduced to meet "competition." The distortion became more acute and raised a lot of controversy when the so-called 50-50 Formula was introduced to the Middle East in 1950 and the oil-producing countries became conscious of the price level.

Throughout the 1950s the oil-producing nations, dealing individually with the oil companies, were faced with an overwhelming monopolistic power. In the First Arab Petroleum Congress, held in Cairo after a price reduction, a resolution was passed specifying that price alteration by a company should take place only after discussions with the governments of petroleum-exporting countries. When the companies reduced oil prices for the second time on 9 August 1960, the month-old OPEC moved. On 10 September its first resolution strongly expressed collective concern about pricing and urged the companies to restore prices to previous levels and maintain them steady and free from unnecessary fluctuations.

During the 1960s, OPEC barely succeeded in holding out, in face of the companies' forceful attacks, raising its per barrel take by a few cents through so-called royalty expensing. OPEC's failure to restore prices to their previous level was due mainly to a persistent oversupply, which was partly an outcome of market structure and behavior. A shut-in capacity of nearly 25 percent on a world scale was kept by the companies, apparently in conformity with one of the recommendations passed by the Ministerial Council of OEEC after the 1956 Suez crisis. Other recommendations were aimed at safeguarding the interests of western countries by urging the companies to intensify exploration activities west of Suez (hence the development of North Africa, the North Sea, and Alaska), enlarge storage capacity in the consuming countries, and build larger tankers to be routed around Africa with costs competitive with the Suez route.

Summary of OPEC Grievances

The failure of OPEC to increase prices during the 1960s, however, was counterbalanced by its success in preventing further reduction by the companies that claimed that oil in fact was sold in the open market at lower than the posted prices. To summarize OPEC grievances:

1. The posted price of marker crude oil (Arabian 34°) dropped from $2.18 a barrel in 1947 to $1.80 in 1960 where it remained unchanged until the Teheran Agreement of 1971 allowed for a slight increase.

During the same period, the GNP price index for the eighteen industrialized nations of OECD increased from 100 in 1947 to 260 in 1970. More specifically, the price index of manufactured goods exported by OECD members, who accounted for nearly 85 percent of total OPEC imports, had increased during the 1960s by an average rate of 3 percent per year. As a result of the above two factors, the price of oil, in real terms, had been eroded from $2.18 in 1947 to nearly 69 cents in 1970; a drop of over two-thirds.

2. The fall in oil prices was coupled with a fall in transportation costs, an advantage the companies transferred forward to the oil-importing countries rather than backward to the oil-exporting countries. Thus, oil imported by OECD countries during the 1960s fell from $21.32 per ton (Cif) to $16.04 per ton, for a reduction of nearly 25 percent.

3. The share of the price of petroleum received by the oil-exporting countries sold to European consumers during the 1960s at no time exceeded 8 percent of its final price. In comparison, the governments and companies of the oil-consuming countries received around 55 percent of the price in the form of government taxes and company profits, the rest being actual costs. Even after the 1973 price increases, almost one-half of what the consumer pays for oil goes to the public treasuries of consuming countries in the form of various taxes. In 1975, the total sales receipts of a composite barrel averaged $33.20 in Western Europe in the following shares: $14.90 (or 45 percent) by governments of consuming countries, $10.10 (or 30 percent) by oil-exporting countries, and the rest ($8.20) represented the companies' profits and costs.

Another version of the same grievance may be shown by the present widening gap between OPEC official prices and market prices. During the second half of 1979, spot market prices for the marker crude have soared to more than double the official price, as have prices of oil products in the spot market. Much of the gain has gone to profiteers, while the oil producers were left with the blame. No wonder some OPEC members have begun to use techniques that would either inhibit profiteering or allow them to share in the excess profits.

4. In their pre-1973 attempt to improve their share of total oil revenue, oil exporters had been trying hard to push forward their goal through negotiation with companies. As mentioned earlier, ten years of tough negotiation throughout the 1960s succeeded in increasing OPEC governments' take by only a few cents per barrel, which then was offset in real terms by

creeping inflation. Despite a partial rectification by the Teheran and Geneva Agreements in the early 1970s, the distortion continued due to an accelerating rate of inflation. The governments' income continued to dwindle in real terms until the whole system was ignited by the spark of war in October 1973. In two months the governments' take jumped from $2 to $9 a barrel.

No sooner had oil prices been rectified than the course of events again worked against oil exporters. Between 1974 and the last quarter of 1978, OPEC's terms of trade with the industrialized nations worsened. The official price index of marker crude rose during this period from 100 to 116.6, while the price index for manufactured goods imported by OPEC (as expressed in U.S. dollars and weighted by the share of each industrial nation in OPEC's imports) rose from 100 to 150. Taking the effect of both inflation and currency fluctuation (that is, drop in the U.S. dollar in which oil prices are posted), oil prices should have gone up at the end of 1978 by some 30 percent above actual level just to preserve the terms of trade at their 1974 level.

5. Oil exporters are often blamed by western sources for all evils suffered by the world economy. One highly publicized area is inflation—an epidemic problem of industrial countries long before the oil crisis. Some studies indicate that even when oil prices were increased fourfold in 1973, oil was not responsible for more than one or two points out of the 13 percent average rate of inflation of 1974. The remainder, or nearly 11 percent, is explained by other factors of western economies. Further confirming this fact is that, despite the freezing of oil prices from October 1975 to January 1977, inflation rates in western countries continued to be high.

Soaring inflation rates eroded not only oil prices as mentioned earlier, but also financial assets. By the end of 1978 nearly $170 billion accumulated by OPEC due to inadequate absorptive capacity had been deposited or recycled into the western financial system. Due to rampant inflation, these financial assets' real value eroded 30 percent by the end of 1978. Moreover, since nearly 70 percent of these financial assets were denominated in U.S. dollars, and since many OPEC countries bought the largest share of their imports from countries with strong currencies, it was estimated the dollar's declining value had caused another 12 percent erosion. A combined drop in the real value of OPEC financial assets has been estimated at 42 percent between 1974 and 1978. For a valuable and depleting resource like oil, such a drop in real value runs against sound economics.

6. Is oil capable of bridging the energy gap through a transition period until sufficient energy alternatives are developed? Recent studies range in outcome from the gloomiest to grey, but seldom rosy. A long-range study by IIASA estimates world energy needs at 35 tetrawatt-years per year by 2030—equivalent to nearly 500 million barrels per day of oil, or four times

the current energy consumption. Both oil and gas, which account now for nearly two-thirds of world energy needs, will not account for more than 14 percent by 2030. The message is quite clear: petroleum is rapidly heading towards zero share, and a period of fifty years is not beyond OPEC's time spectrum.

Even with a shorter spectrum of time, recent studies have escalated downward future expectations for oil and gas. A Central Intelligency Agency study released in August 1979 outlines the difficulty of the decreasing rate of new oil discoveries. During the 1970s world oil production is estimated to have totaled nearly 200 billion barrels, while new discoveries are estimated at only 100 billion—an erosion of nearly one-sixth of world's proven reserves. A Shell Oil Company study presented to the Tenth World Petroleum Congress, September 1979, indicates that the cost to discover and develop new oil resources is expected to skyrocket to ten to twenty times its current level by 2000. As most rich deposits seem to have been already discovered, the world will have to explore the most difficult areas and resort to costly tertiary recovery methods, all with capital costs that range between $20 to $30 thousand per barrels per day capacity (at 1978 dollars). This is to be compared with today's lowest capital costs that range around $2000.

Faced with such an outlook, how would you determine your production levels and at what price would you produce the marginal barrel? Oil exporters were up to their responsibility as to level of production. They have been rapidly depleting their energy resources to meet world requirements and help bridge the gap. OPEC's current development investments plus domestic oil needs, by 1977 standards, required a production level of only 17.7 million barrels per day, while actual production was leveling in that year at 31.4 million barrels per day—a phenomenon that had characterized all years since 1974.

7. The history of hydrocarbons consumption in western countries still reflects wasteful use. Pricing of oil at such low levels prior to the 1970s led to substitution of oil for coal as a low-value fuel. Early in the 1960s, only 30 percent of Britain's coal (then 200 million tons) could compete with oil. Britain had to impose a fuel oil tax of 25 percent in order to support its national coal industry. Japan and West Germany did the same. However, oil continued to replace coal, though at a slower rate. As a result, from 1950 to 1975, the share of coal in world energy consumption fell from 61 percent to 33 percent, while oil rose from 27 percent to 44 percent and natural gas from 10 percent to 20 percent. The change in both Western Europe and Japan was more dramatic. The share of coal dropped from 85 percent in both areas to 25 percent in Western Europe and to 20 percent in Japan. Oil and gas made up for the drop, climbing to 72 percent in Western Europe and to 76.5 percent in Japan.

With the 1973 oil price hike, alternative sources of energy received a great push, and the outlook for both coal and nuclear energy soared. But as time went by and oil markets reflected symptoms of glut and decreasing real prices, the consuming countries regained a sense of relaxation and complacency. Hence, most energy resources were escalated down with the exception of oil, which continued to be considered as a residual fuel. OPEC countries have been called on to produce more than they would otherwise do.

For nuclear power in the non-Communist world, forecasts were reduced during the period from 1973 to 1978, as follows (in gigawatts):

For 1980   from 264 to 146

For 1985   from 257 to 178

For 1990   from 1070 to 500-700

For 2000   from 2000-2500 to 1500-1800

For coal, a number of technological and environmental problems have been recognized; thus, great hopes of a vast resource began to shrink. Best estimates now allow coal in the United States to rise between 1976 and 1990 from 600 million tons to 1400, and for Western Europe, a negligible increase from 327 to 345 million tons.

Other long-range studies by the World Energy Conference expect world coal production to rise between 1976 and 2020 from 2.7 billion tons to 8.7 at a growth rate of 2.7 percent per year, or almost the same as the 2.6 percent average of the period from 1960 to 1975.[1]

8. There has been significant waste of natural gas produced in the form of associated and dissolved gas. Because low oil prices did not justify gas liquefaction and ocean transport in the past, it was flared. It is not known how much wealth was wasted over more than four decades, but oil producers paid heavily for this loss. Even now, quantities of gas equivalent to 2.5 million barrels per day of oil are flared each day in OPEC countries. This amount corresponds to one and one-half times the predicted combined output of synthetic oil to be extracted from shale, tar sands, and coal in 1990.

Oil-importing countries are emphasizing development of costly indigenous sources of energy and refusing to let gas prices increase to a level that would allow a fair return on investment. Certainly, the level of gas pricing that would provide incentives for liquefaction and conservation is still lower than the cost of developing all alternative sources of energy. This is again a case of deviation from sound economics.

9. Another grievance of OPEC centers on the shift of refineries from the exporting to the importing countries. Taking Arab oil exports alone, which in 1977 amounted to nearly 56 percent of total world exports, the ratio of crude oil to total exports was as high as 93 percent.

Western Europe and Japan chose to import oil in crude form after World War II and built refineries at home. Hence, their combined refining capacity rose between 1940 and 1977 from one-half million barrels per day (8 percent of the non-Communist world) to 26 million barrels per day (40 percent). By contrast, OPEC with 66 percent of non-Communist world production had only 8 percent of its refining capacity by the end of 1977, with the Arab countries accounting for a disproportionate 3.7 percent.

The refining industry is a crucial element in any development process. During years of recent negotiation under the Euro-Arab dialogue, we have failed to convince the European Economic Community (EEC) to lower barriers against Arab oil products. More recently, there has been more readiness to shut in some of the excess capacity and abstain from building new European capacity in favor of the Arab oil products. This positive move was not without price; certain supply concessions were requested in return.

10. Since OPEC members are earnestly trying to turn their financial assets into productive capital assets, they focus attention on the problem of transfer of technology. Transfer, assimilation, and adaptation of technology have not been easy for developing nations. With oil becoming an increasingly scarce resource, OPEC will have to use it as leverage to attain its goals.

One fortunate phenomenon has been the changing role of the oil multinationals. To their classical role as international oil and gas traders, some of them have recently added the roles of investor and provider of those services and technologies that are most needed for development. Conservation of energy is an important area in technology transfer and one of vital interest for both consumers and producers of oil. This implies the improvement of economic and technical efficiency through structural changes in production, transformation, and consumption of energy.

In conclusion, I want to ask: Are those people on the other side of the fence without a case to listen to and discuss? Are the leaders of OPEC just arrogant sheiks who refuse to talk, or are they responsible statesmen and businessmen who want fair deals and want to be treated on a footing of equality? I will leave the bottom line for you to draw.

Note

1. L. Grainger, ed., *Energy Resources: Availability and Rational Use: A Digest of the Tenth World Energy Conference, Istanbul, 19-23 September 1977* (Guilford, England: IPC Science and Technology Press, 1978).

10 Attitudes toward the United States

Ragaei El Mallakh

My concern is the attitude of OPEC and non-OPEC nations toward the United States, specifically in the area of economics and finance. It is misleading to deal with OPEC as if it were one single entity. The reasons for the success and durability of OPEC are the fact that it allowed, and will continue to allow, a great deal and sense of flexibility. This flexibility allows different views from those who are moderate members of OPEC and from those who are extremists in their policies toward pricing and output.

There is tremendous emphasis among some of the oil producers toward conservation of output because the future of all producers (OPEC and non-OPEC countries, moderate and so-called radical members) is dependent on the lengthening of the period of the utilization of oil, not only in selling it abroad but also in using it at home for industrialization and agricultural development.

The OPEC countries vary tremendously in their policy not only toward their own resources, but also toward their contribution to world stability and orderly development, in particular, avoidance of severe recession or depression in the West. The fact that Saudi Arabia, or the United Arab Emirates, or the State of Qatar continue to produce two-thirds more than they actually need to meet their financial requirements is indicative of their attitude toward the world's orderly development and avoidance of upheavals that, of course, could affect them. But their feeling that they belong to such a world is much more pronounced than our feeling that they share our interests and our development.

At the International Research Center for Energy and Economic Development, we have been examining the concept of absorptive capacity of these countries. What is meant by *absorptive capacity?* It refers to the internal level of investment that could be carried out with acceptable rates of return. Rates of return are decided by governments in most of these countries. So social, as well as political and economic, factors have to be taken into account. The low absorbers, three of which I just mentioned, want one thing: that we help them to absorb rationally their oil-generated funds.

We have neglected to examine the impact of such investments on the distribution of income and on inflation; rather, we have concentrated on the rate of return as if these countries were business entities that do not have anything to consider but the actual dividends or rate of profit. The issue is more involved, and I think one of the reasons for the failure of the former system of Iran is the fact that the absorptive capacity was rapidly expanded, or more capital funds were absorbed, without adequate concern about the effect of such investments on the rate of inflation, the distribution of income, the rate of urbanization, and the like.

There are countries, such as Algeria and Libya, that are more resistant to higher prices. Their oil reserves are much more limited proportionately than those of Saudi Arabia, the United Arab Emirates, or Kuwait.

As a group, OPEC does have grievances. I have been attending OPEC seminars for the last three years; interestingly enough, western representatives at these seminars keep quiet like mice because they want to be invited again and they seem to feel an element of guilt.

In connection with absorptive capacity, one has to consider refining and petrochemicals as an essential part of the future of these nations. Two or three years ago, we were telling these OPEC countries they could not develop petrochemicals because there is a poor market for petrochemicals. What can we tell them right now? These are issues for which solutions have to be found in order to allow for orderly development in these countries and, of course, this is reflected in our own economic system.

There has been tremendous discrimination against investment from these countries in the United States—not only in the area of federal government controls and regulations, but also from local and state governments. While Canadian money is coming here, some German money, and so on, certain sectors of our economy are reluctant to accept Middle Eastern capital funds. So what alternative is left for these countries? How could we ask Saudi Arabia, for example, to continue producing 9.5 million barrels per day if we restrict the Saudi investment in this country?

In improving international relations with the OPEC oil producers, the United States has to consider many such financial aspects and economic development issues in order to achieve some element of stability that is sorely needed.

11 The Lack of a U.S. Energy Policy

Eric Zausner

When we talk about domestic energy policy and its foreign ramifications, I have sympathy for the producers who own the oil and have a right to try to price it in the market and set a production level consistent with their own economic development policies. To the extent that there is a problem, it is of our own making; it is caused by the consuming countries.

The reality is that we do not have an effective energy program in the United States. Notwithstanding all the rhetoric on moral equivalents of war, project independences, and national energy plans, and so forth, we do not have an effective program.

There is no question that overdependence is a compellingly difficult problem for the United States. We have a situation where our import bill has gone from something like $2 billion to $80 billion in eight or ten years and is rapidly heading into the $100 to $200 billion annual range. This is a tremendous tax on our economy, a tremendous transfer of wealth. Like it or not, our dependence on suppliers from the Middle East countries has gone up staggeringly in the last five or six years. It was something like 1 million out of 6 million barrels a day imported at the time of the 1973 embargo. In 1980 it was closer to 3.5 or 4 out of 8 or 9 million barrels.

Like it or not, many of those Middle East sources are uncertain—not because they want to be uncertain, but because there are events in that area of the world we can not control and even the countries who supply oil cannot control. In the long term, oil dependence impacts our productivity, the rate of our economic growth, and a number of other things. It is our problem. It was not inherently brought about by the formation of OPEC; nor would it be changed by some magical government entity interposing itself somehow to bring about either more stability or lower prices—neither, in fact, would occur.

The crime—the troubling part—about it is not so much that oil is $37 or $40 a barrel, but the fact that countries like the United States have a myriad of alternatives at substantially lower prices than either $40 today or where $40 is going to be in the next ten years. The crime with respect to our energy policy is the unending wall we have built between the things we can do domestically and what is happening internationally. That goes for both conventional resources of oil and gas, as well as for coal, for renewable resources, be they solar, biomass, or whatever. We have set up a very sophisticated and complex structure standing in the way of replacing $40 oil with lots of domestic alternatives that are either cheaper today or clearly cheaper than expectations with respect to oil. That has very significant consequences, obviously, for our own economy. As important, this obstacle sets up expectations in the world that suggest prices are going to go even higher than they might otherwise be if we were embarking on a domestic program that moved us toward less dependence.

I would like to focus on the more subtle part of the domestic policy. This debate has typically revolved around what the U.S. domestic energy policy can be-the soft path or the hard path, nuclear or coal, or renewables versus nonrenewables.

We have failed to structure a U.S. policy to help stabilize and moderate world-market trends. There is no reason to believe that Mother Nature put all the oil in the Middle East. There are a number of less-developed countries that do not have the financial or technical wherewithal either to locate or develop oil. Even if those countries find that oil, produce it, and price it exactly as OAPEC, the more we help diversify the source of oil, the more countries that provide oil, the more time we are going to buy for the transition, the more we are going to moderate long-term price impacts. We are not doing that.

We argue endlessly about the soft path in the United States. There are tremendous institutional problems, for example, bringing many of those so-called soft-path technologies into our economy where we have a massive capital investment in equipment that uses centralized power sources or oil or gas. That is often not the case in the less-developed countries.

We spend money designing a better solar pool heater. Parts of Africa need solar stoves, and the countries there do not need to face the institutional problems that we have in the United States. One of the things we can do internationally is help many of the less-developed countries to leapfrog the cycle we went through by linking industrialization to heavy energy use. We are not doing that.

We continue to mix up security needs with our energy objectives. If you want to put an embargo on Russia, embargo something that hurts them—not something that hurts us. Not allowing the Russians to have oil field technology can ultimately push them into the world market as an importer rather than an exporter. That hurts us. Doing so will escalate their desire to play a more forceful role in the Middle East. We do not have a policy that differentiates between what we do not want them to have—missiles, wheat, or the Olympics—and what we think they ought to buy from the United States. The list goes on.

The United States does not have a consistent, rational international policy to stabilize world oil markets and temper potential price increases. We can do a tremendous range of things in that regard. While synfuels is an expensive alternative, it is one of the few ways we can ultimately put a cap on oil prices by demonstrating that we can tap shale and coal cleanly and technically as liquid and gaseous fuels. While I have no big desire for a hundred synthetic fuel plants, I would like to see five and know what they cost and prove that they work. I do not really care whether it is $40 or $200 a barrel—the United States must find out what the costs of synfuel technology are. And the list goes on.

The reason we do not have an effective domestic energy program is simple. The politician is not able to deal with situations that exact difficult costs. Each energy choice the United States faces exacts difficult costs. It faces higher prices, harmful environmental impact, or wasteful regional trade-offs for national benefit. There is nothing you can do in the energy area without disrupting the industrial structure in some way.

What makes it so difficult for the political process is not only that the costs are high but also that the benefits are ten years away. We would need to raise gas prices today so tertiary recovery or advanced gas recovery techniques will add gas ten years from now. We are asking political people to exact difficult costs for benefits that are five elections away. That means politicians tend to follow, not lead. We do not even have a national consensus on whether oil overdependence is a serious problem or not; it is not surprising, therefore, that the politician is not leading and does not have much guidance.

I am always amazed by the number of people who have never tried to run an energy program, yet who are absolutely convinced the government can do it either by setting up fifty-three tiers of oil categories or by designing rationing systems, or whatever. The government does those things terribly. The best intentions often do not get translated into action.

One anecdote points up the problems that occur in the best-laid plans. I was in charge of the gasoline rationing program. We decided it was going to be a white market and needed to print coupons. Our economist calculated that the white-market value of each coupon would be somewhere between 25 and 50 cents per gallon of gasoline.

This worried the Treasury Department in terms of counterfeiting. There are two ways to avoid counterfeiting: make the coupon difficult to reproduce and make it so a counterfeit is easily recognizable, something that people can detect at a glance. We decided to print in the center of each coupon an exact replica of George Washington as used on a one-dollar bill. Its complexity would make it hard to counterfeit, and a blatant counterfeit would be easy to determine. We printed 4.6 billion gasoline coupons. Then we found out that the center of the dollar bill, George Washington, is what makes dollar-bill changing machines release a dollar in coins. So, in our infinite wisdom, to prevent counterfeiters from making 50 cents on a 50-cent coupon, we made them worth a dollar.

I do not want my oil delivered the way we deliver the mail, and I do not think anybody else does either. The energy system is horribly complex and dynamic. The government, and it does not matter whether it has 3,000 bureaucrats or 10,000, cannot deal with that complexity very well. It tends to take snapshots—to try to fix problems where it finds them. But the system keeps changing and moving and new problems crop up.

The government is also not very good in long-range planning. In my particular office, when we got through to the next Friday, I considered it relatively visionary. That does not work too well in energy. We are reacting to gasoline shortages; we are reacting to Three Mile Islands; we are not setting a long-term comprehensive policy to deal with long-term issues. The government has not been successful at finding opportunities to replace that oil dependence with economically sound domestic sources.

Questions and Answers to Part IV

Question: Dr. Abdallah, would you comment on the outlook for production capacity expansion among some of the core OPEC countries such as Saudi Arabia?

Answer: I care more about analyzing forces than figures because past history actually shows figures can differ from expectations alone. Expectations differ about the Saudis' intention as to developing their capacity. I feel they would not really be in favor of large-scale development of their capacity because there are now concerns about being pressed by the West to produce more than they should.

Question: Dr. El Mallakh and Dr. Abdallah, would you address the possibility of OPEC taking a greater role and a greater share of investment capacity in the less-developed countries?

Answer: (Dr. El Mallakh) OPEC has its own special fund, enlargement of which has been recently suggested, to devote $1.6 billion for economic aid to the less-developed countries. This is double the $800 million allocated last year. There is no doubt that more could be done in the area of assistance. Two very important points are here. First, Arab states are broadening their aid program to include nonregional countries; now Latin American, African, and Asian nations are recipients of such aid. Second, the aid element of the loans is a higher percentage than the aid given by either the western bloc or the eastern bloc; the aid itself is carried out with a very low rate of interest or service charge and for a longer period, which allows these countries to develop according to their requirements and resources.

Answer: (Dr. Abdallah) Oil producers who have financial assets are not really free to spend their money and give it away—maybe because the financial system would not really allow the transformation of such financial assets in a short time into physical assets which would in that case be a real burden on the balance of payment. Again, the interests of some of these countries are associated more with the western countries than with the developing countries.

OPEC oil earnings are not permanent or stable but fluctuate. It depends upon the depletion of a natural resource; it is not a permanent rate, as it is in the industrialized countries. So, in fact, the whole issue is complex. In general, OPEC potential to take greater share in investing in the less-developed countries is limited, not only by its inability to mobilize financial assets in great quantities, but also by the instability of its earnings.

Question: (by Yahia Abdul-Rahman) We need an atmosphere of cooperation, not confrontation. I do not see why the West cannot develop the Middle East economies in an orderly manner acceptable to the Middle East countries' aspirations. It is going to be a matter of more efficient recycling of oil dollars in a way that is going to bring prosperity to the people of the Middle East. The question I have for Dr. Abdallah is, Are there any cultural barriers between the OPEC countries as producers and consumers on the western side of the hemisphere?

Answer: The oil countries' energy decision makers' natural inclination is toward the West, and they would like to do business, but they want it to be done on a footing of equality. In OAPEC we have held four international seminars since 1974—one in London, one in Paris, one in Tokyo, one in Oslo, and one at the University of Wisconsin. Participating in all these seminars were groups of the industrialized countries, some energy people, and some bankers and industrialists. The dialogue was going fine—exchange of views, objectives, and everybody on our side—in particular, the oil industry was there and expressed its views.

I will tell you one secret: when we were discussing whether or not to hold one seminar in the United States, some members were hesitant because they felt the media in the United States hold a hostile attitude toward foreign oil production and would not give them fair coverage. However, we overcame the idea and held a seminar at the University of Wisconsin, where it was mainly attended by scholars and professors.

Question: (by Yahia Abdul-Rahman) Eric Zausner, having been to the Middle East and being an international traveler, do you have any ideas along these lines?

Answer: In the last couple of years we have lived on borrowed time. We had deluded ourselves that the OPEC absorptive capacity was much higher than it truly was. We congratulated ourselves, particularly in the early 1970s, on our ability to sell more to the Middle East countries.

What we found is that what we sold OPEC was not really what they needed, that the infusion often was military equipment, that massive inflation was caused in these countries, that social change was being forced—all out of proportion to the benefit. And I think what has happened in Iran has been only a more rapid, more violent change. But the prophetic writing was on the wall—the lower absorptive capacity, intense pressures caused by westernization, increased standard of living—we were trying to use those resources more rapidly than was wise. These pressures not only changed the Iranian view, but also all of the Middle Eastern producers' views about the problems of trying to absorb change and the use of those funds at a very rapid rate.

We may never again see higher production than we are seeing today coming out of the Middle East countries. And even that production, as pointed out earlier, is far above the minimum needed in an absorptive sense. The Mexicans are saying much the same thing, that there will be a balance on setting production levels between the demands of the western world and the needs of those countries to use those resources. It is no longer true that those countries will do what we need. Now we are going to see a different process of how the producers weigh the level at which they are going to produce, and they are going to be tempering our demands by their realities. That is a very significant change—and one that we are going to have to accept and recognize as a viable balance and reasonable perspective.

Question: Dr. Abdallah, do you feel there is a valid economic basis for OPEC petrochemical production, considering the kind of scale that is necessary and the complexity of the basic oil and downstream units?

Answer: Retrospectively, if the resources had been in the hands of the producing countries from the 1940s on (when the petrochemical industry was just starting), there was a chance, I think, to participate. But, of course, after petrochemical processing capacity was built somewhere else. . . .

Question: Excuse me. Your presumption is that petrochemical overcapacity in Europe and Japan and the United States prevents Middle East production. The numbers that we have looked at, even if everything was given in terms of energy and hydrocarbons, show that you simply could not compete. It was not an economic proposition, and there are reasons for that: production would be thousands of miles from where petrochemicals will be used, technical service laboratories would also be very far from the customers, and institutional problems exist to prevent you from being very successful.

Answer: (Dr. El Mallakh) There are really three points I would like to refer to. One is the dynamic aspect of competitive advantage. Initially Middle Eastern producers are not going to do well. It will take time for them to get their foot in the market, so to speak. The second point is that they have the capital funds available, and the West does not. And the third point is that nobody is talking about manufacturing a complete inventory of petrochemicals. One can choose the so-called mature types, the types that require a great deal of natural gas and oil, less processing, yet are capital intensive.

There are already examples of success—specifically, in Bahrain, a plastics industry. The energy-intensive industries in the Persian or Arab Gulf have been basically successful. The Middle East could become an aluminum smelting production center, being centrally located with regard to the Far East, Europe, Africa, and so on. It is not necessarily going to replace all the production centers around the world, particularly in the ones that you have in mind.

Answer: (Yahia Abdul-Rahman) What we are concerned with here, I think, is the cyclical behavior of the marketplace. If you look at any refinery in the West and at its profitability as a function of time, as perceived when it was designed and put in place, and what happened later on, you will find that the refinery rides with the cycle. But if you talk about so-called inflation index pricing and extrapolation on a straight-line fashion, you will never have an economically sound project, whether in the OPEC countries, in the United States, or Western Europe. Now, you have to make the strategic decision: whether you want to go ahead with something or not. OPEC has to decide, to take the risk, because the business of extrapolating a straight line into the future has proved to be a failure and misleading.

Question: What I hear you proposing is that we are entering a new era of cooperation for the mutual benefit of East and West. My question concerns your feeling of the political direction of the OPEC or Gulf States.

In the early 1970s, the discussion centered around the extent to which the producing countries would be allowed to take a larger role in the production, aiming toward 51 percent. One speaker, Mr. Yamani, referred to this 51 percent as a partnership, akin to a Catholic marriage. A question from the audience asked: "I thought a Catholic marriage was a 50-50 proposition—how do you reconcile this with the 51 percent?" The immediate response was, "This is an Islamic-Catholic marriage." Would you respond to that?

Answer: (Dr. Abdallah) Actually, it is a matter of history, and things have to be judged at the time. The introduction of joint participation by the independent companies after World War II was a great improvement over the concession system. In the early 1960s, the OPEC world was just trying to organize. The exchange of credentials with the United Nations as an intergovernmental organization was something big to celebrate. And in the 1960s, one cent or so was a great price increase. So it has to be judged within the framework of the evolution. The fact that the companies had been there from the 1920s, when the Arab world was a group of backward, undeveloped countries, does not mean that this relationship would not evolve. Even in marriage, if the relationship does not evolve, it dies. So this 51 percent could be okay at one time, but later 100 percent would be satisfactory.

Answer: (Dr. El Mallakh) I agree with Dr. Abdallah. But whether it is Catholic or not, they are still living together; there has not been any divorce or separation.

**Part V
Social/Economic and
Environmental Impacts of
Alternative Energy Sources**

Introduction to Part V

Edward Myers, Jr.

As responsible, obligated suppliers of electric energy, our power and light companies once had a good 100-year-long record of service, before we started getting so much help from so many of our friends. Americans are comfortable with their energy habits today and with their energy institutions. They still look to these institutions to a great degree to help solve their energy future. Of course, people as a rule tend to fight change, and there is in this optimistic America of ours a rather great burgeoning hope that there are easy solutions and that we can return to the previous era of abundance and cheap energy.

But the only mechanism for improved efficiency and return to those earlier halcyon days lies in the heart of each one of us, because our institutions are hopelessly confounded. Energy institutions seek conventional responses. In utilities, large centralized energy production with elaborate distribution schemes have worked for a long time, they have in the past supplied abundant and cheap energy, and we are loath to walk away from them. We tend to rely on centralized energy sources: petroleum, natural gas, coal, nuclear.

Words like *conservation* and *soft energy* are new and somewhat frightening in our business. California is blessed with a forward-looking regulatory pressure that has gotten its utilities into the energy services business, ownership of cogeneration plants, development of solar energy plants and the installation of consumer solar sources, development of geothermal steam fields, and establishment of pioneer windmills as early as ten years ago.

But despite such a forward look, American energy institutions are meeting much resistance because the prices are going up—and we have seen nothing yet to show how far they will go. Partly responsible is the production of waste, which continues to be anathema to the average citizen.

12 The Least-Cost Energy Strategy

Roger Sant

My desire is to be optimistic, because I think the energy data we have developed in the last couple of years lead to that conclusion. Our current situation is like the good news/bad news jokes: the good news is that there is plenty of gasoline down at the gas station, and the bad news is that the only currency they will take is gold Krugerrands; or the good news is that we have a new secretary of energy, and the bad news is that we still need a secretary of energy.

The bad news about energy has been with us for a while. Imports are up, with the 1980 bill perhaps some $83 billion; the Middle East is in turmoil, we probably are going to be living in fear of disruption, Soviet production of oil has peaked, and on and on. The bad news about energy has been articulated to the point where I think American consumers are scared because they do not know what to do. There is a sense of powerlessness which we as a country have felt after receiving that information. We do not seem to know or feel that we can do anything.

Now the good news is that all of the economic forces in the United States are heading toward a solution. I did not say the market is progressing toward a solution, but that all the economic forces that we can find are progressing toward an equilibrium in which this energy crunch all works out. It may not look that way right now, and certainly it is not being told that way, but the evidence is there.

If, since the embargo in 1973, we had done what the economics of energy indicated we should have done, we would probably be close to a solution right now. By solution, I mean energy would not be an issue on which we need a conference or that it would not be something about which to worry. And even though we have not done what the economics would indicate we should have done, economic forces are still heading toward a natural solution.

In fact, 1979 may have been the first year in which we really have some evidence of that. Oil consumption was down significantly, natural gas consumption was up, electricity was unchanged to down, coal was just a little up, and efficiency was way up. That is the first year in which you could recount the things that happened and say those are what the economic forces would indicate should have happened. Prior to that, there did not even seem to be evidence that the forces that were at work were working the way they ought to.

The Consumer's Point of View

Now how do we reach the conclusion that things might work out? The most important thing is to shift our focus from Btus, or barrels, or imports to what the U.S. consumer looks at. For 220 million American people energy is not abstract. It is seen in terms of very tangible benefits that we receive each day. Energy is a comfortable room, a lighted desk, cooked food, or a television picture that works, or a seat in a vehicle that moves down a highway. Or, if you are an industrialist, it is a 2200-degree temperature that makes steel such that you can work with it. These benefits all of us get from energy are not being addressed.

Those of us who are in the politics of energy have tended to look at Btus, kilowatt-hours, therms, cubic feet, barrels, all of which are very remote from the average person's perception of what he gets from energy; to that consumer, energy is nothing more than a means to an end. It is the benefits that we need to look at.

The goal in our national energy policy was never to focus on the consumer, and it never was a program to provide the benefits at the lowest possible cost. We focused on imports, on mandatory shifting of fuels, on thermostat turn-downs, on fifty-five-mile-per-hour speed limits, carpooling, and leaving your car home once a week—all of the things that President Carter spoke about when he talked about conservation. All of us are scared because that is not the way we want our lives to be.

This may explain why the public has had such an apathetic reaction to the messages of three presidents, ever since the embargo. There is a sense that we are not doing anything for the consumer. It is fascinating that when the light bulb was invented by Thomas Edison, it was not sold in terms of kilowatt-hours; it was sold in terms of light-hours, and you paid so much per light-hour. That is a fairly tangible benefit; a light bulb lights up and you pay for it on an hourly basis. Edison was just livid when we shifted to selling kilowatt-hours, which people could not understand and which took all the incentive away from improving the light bulb.

Least-Cost Energy Strategy

In 1979, we at the Energy Productivity Center decided to see if we could focus on the practical objective of providing everyone the energy services he wants at the lowest possible cost. We called it the "least-cost energy strategy," and said we wanted to test it as a hypothesis. If you need to get a constituency about energy, you work with cost, because that is on the public's mind. Therefore, a lot of politicians, missing the point completely decided that we should control prices. What people want is to be assured that they can have what they need at the lowest possible cost. We decided to test the economics in such a way that we could determine what the economic forces would do if we could allow that to happen.

Even the process was interesting to me, because I learned some things. For instance, energy expenditures for operating appliances and making hot water were more than the fuel costs for automobiles in 1978. The cost of running electric motors in industry was two and one-half times that of the cost of generating steam. The cost of energy in industry was almost one-half of the cost of energy in buildings. The energy expense in buildings was more than that in transportation. We got all sorts of information from looking at the expenditures for energy that we never got from looking at the Btus of energy. The only time a Btu is a Btu is when it is heating water one degree, and that is the only time when gas or coal or electricity are the same. From then on, Btus are different, and yet, our accounting system assumes they are the same.

Our first discovery was that some of the results were very surprising. We compared 1978 as it actually occurred; that is, we assumed that all of the benefits required in 1978 in terms of heat for rooms and end-use benefits were needed by the economy and that we could not reduce the level of service. In other words, we did not try to cut down on the amount of driving; we did not try to turn down the thermostats; we did not try to reduce production. So our case was a hypothetical test: if we provided those same benefits at the least possible cost using the best available technology, what would be the outcome?

Several Uncompetitive Areas

The outcome was startling. In 1978 we were paying roughly $16 a barrel for imported oil and, according to what we found in our limited investigation, about half of that was uncompetitive (that is, it was not the least-cost option in providing the level of services we wanted). Even at those lower, outdated prices, oil was uncompetitive, and it tells us the domestic opportunities for competing with OPEC are substantially better than we have been thinking.

Surprisingly, 43 percent of the electricity generated centrally was not competitive. That means that at the prices charged in 1978 for electricity, 43 percent of the electricity used was not the least-cost way of providing the services that people were asking for. Who would have said that before?

One-third of the coal used directly (not burned to generate electricity) in industry was not competitive. Natural gas—we might get a clue from the way it is priced—was underutilized relative to its economics. We ought to have been using about 12 percent more natural gas in 1978 that we actually did. Interestingly, that is exactly what happened in 1979. And the tech-

nologies that improve efficiency—better insulation, recuperators, cogeneration—could satisfy about one-third of our total demand for services at the
least cost.

The total result of the whole calculus was that, if we had been able to
achieve this hypothetical result, the cost to the consumer would have been
reduced by roughly $200 per capita, or a total of $43 billion for the
economy. That number would be substantially larger with 1979 prices.

Some other results are these: industry's use of natural gas should have
been about 50 percent higher than it was in 1978. In other words, industry
was underutilizing gas by about 50 percent in terms of a least-cost alternative. And building use was just the opposite, about twice as high as it
should have been. If there were a way now for industry to install conservation or efficiency in buildings, that would make gas the cheapest fuel they
could buy. Industry, of course, would like to buy more natural gas if it
could be confident of supply. The supply is available in the building sector
where it is being overused, and we need to retrofit buildings in existence to
make it the cheapest gas we can find.

Two-thirds of the resultant reduction in electricity can be achieved by
the replacement of large power generation with small power generation
where we can utilize the waste heat. The key to doing this is called *cogeneration*; any time you can use waste heat in an electrical generating process,
you generally come out with an attractive economic result. Only one-third
of the reduction we experienced came directly from the efficient use of electricity.

We found that the efficiency improvements indicated by the 1978
economics would carry us to 1990 if all we did was keep current production
and all the conventional fuels at the same level. At those current levels, at
those indicated results, one can only come out saying, "Who ever put upon
us the notion that there is a scarce energy situation here? Who ever said that
because some oil is not available there is a scarce energy situation in the
United States?"

Combinations and Permutations

We found many different combinations and many different choices. What
is described here is just one of the possible outcomes. So many choices are
available, all of which are more attractive than what we were doing, that
one could not even begin to argue that we have a scarcity situation. And certainly one could not argue that we should control prices because there is a
monopoly in oil, gas, or electricity. There is so much competition among
those three fuels in so many different ways we are missing the point completely if we try to control their prices.

Here are some of the interesting specific investments: $93 billion were cost-effective to invest in the known technologies that can improve chassis and power-train technologies in automobiles; $88 billion were called for to retrofit existing residential structures; $56 billion in industrial gas turbine cogeneration, assuming the gas were to be made available from the residential and commercial structures; $21 billion in diesel automobiles, which is already going on; $20 billion in structural improvements in commercial buildings; $18 billion in cogeneration in small buildings; $10 billion in improved efficiency of electric motors. The total was $364 billion that were cost-effective could be invested in improving the efficiency with which we use our primary fuels.

So, if you look at the situation as an opportunity and not as a problem, that is a large number; $364 billion can be translated into market opportunities, not lost in terms of a scarcity situation! Already, about $360 billion have been invested in the energy sector since 1972, and that number just happens to coincide with what I used as cost-effective in terms of investing in improved efficiency. However, the trouble is that two-thirds of the $360 billion spent has gone to build power plants. In other words, about $270 billion have been invested in power plants since 1972, and about one-third of the $360 billion has been invested in oil, gas, and coal. Those are rough numbers but maybe only 2 percent has been spent on improved efficiency.

So far, the indication is that the market is not working right, or else our numbers are completely wrong—and that could be true. But the indication at this point is that, in spite of our joy in our economy, in allocating capital, we have a pretty sad record of what we have purchased. But that is starting to turn around. There was strong evidence of that in 1979. Certainly the investment in power plants has started to decline. Industry is now getting through the initial stages of housekeeping function improvements that have been extremely effective and is now looking solidly at some investments.

Exciting New Developments

Some exciting products are beginning to be offered. There is a company called Scallop Thermal Management Company in New York, a subsidiary of Shell Oil Company, that is actually selling heat and hot water, not fuel oil. You can contract to have a seventy-degree office, and they take the risk of degree days. You can buy heat; you do not have to buy fuel oil, and in the process they improve the furnace, building insulation, controls so that you get heat at the lowest possible cost they can provide it—and the same thing for hot water. Interestingly, about 70 percent of the commercial buildings in France now utilize this sort of contract, and Scallop, the company that began it, is now in the United States offering the same thing.

The fastest growing energy company right now is Honeywell, Inc. They are growing about 28 or 29 percent a year; something like 65 percent of their business is directly energy related. With all of their control experience, the Honeywell people now believe that a 40 percent savings in commercial buildings is so normal they are willing to guarantee the outcome. They are talking about offering a contract for complete energy service—heat, light, hot water, and other functions—such that Honeywell would take the responsibility for managing, installing, and investing to get a building to an optimal state.

General Public Utilities, which may be in the worst shape of any utility in the country after the Three Mile Island accident, has decided that, because of capital scarcity, the only thing they can do to increase capacity is to invest the few dollars they have in improved efficiency and load management. They have proposed to the New Jersey Public Utilities Commission and to the Pennsylvania Public Utilities Commission that they be allowed to invest in home retrofit, storage devices that will improve their load factor, improved electric motors, cogeneration, and so on. They asked their commission if they can put the cost of everything that will be cheaper than the cost of a new electric power plant in their rate base, just as they would the cost of a new power plant.

The optimism of the 1980s, I suspect, is that by 1990 consumers will have what they are crying for now: choice. The choices available now, such as solar and conservation, are not quite developed to the point where people feel confident they are good investments. But by the end of the 1980s, the choices will be there, the competition will be there, and the electric utilities will probably be offering light-hours or light and heat and hot water again instead of selling kilowatt-hours.

New companies like Honeywell will be selling all sorts of services. The new product opportunities will be immense. My guess is that the total consumer cost of service will not be any higher in real terms than now. There will be such tremendous opportunities for substitution at costs so attractive that, overall, the cost of energy services will not rise in real terms over the next decade. And oil companies, perhaps, will do much the same as what we see now, investing in utilization technologies such as electric motors.

What is needed for that happy result? Nothing. What is needed if we want it to happen by 1985 instead of 1990? It certainly is not government. Legislators ought to do everything they can to remove themselves from the scene, rather than try to provide more tax incentives and subsidies, and put the highest priority on filling the strategic reserves in case of disruption between now and then.

You may wonder what is the most exciting new technology for the next few decades. Washington spends a lot of time and dollars on research and development, and the most exciting answer is something already available:

the slow-speed diesel. The big old two-stroke, slow-speed diesel that we have been using in ships for years could run on a coal/water slurry and can cogenerate. Its cost per kilowatt is about one-third that of a new coal or nuclear power plant. Isn't that ironic?

Questions and Answers

Question: You indicated that the market system has not worked very well although the situation is turning around. You implied that maybe the government should be doing something to help us make rational decisions about energy. Could you mention just a few of what those things might be?

Answer: Well, actually that is not my conclusion. I have spent a long time trying to figure out what the government should do to help us make rational decisions. It was very difficult in those early days to get conservation perceived as on a parity with supply investment. If I were to want anything to happen, it would just be a general articulation of that parity, but I cannot see a government program that does the appropriate thing. I think subsidies tend just to get in the way: the 20 percent federal energy tax credit didn't evoke any particular incremental response that we can tell.

So I conclude that the government should get out of the Fuel Use Act—you know that is a crazy piece of legislation. It is forcing people to make decisions to use coal that are totally uneconomic and will not do anything good for us in the long run. Get the government out of the incremental pricing provisions of natural gas. I spent a couple of hours with Senator John Heinz of Pennsylvania recently, because that was just the question he asked: What should we do? And I cannot come up with anything that I would like to urge except let the forces start turning; we're not going to be able to stop them. I am spending all my personal time trying to excite private organizations to respond to the opportunity and am spending no time with Congress.

Question: When you were calculating the least-cost strategy, did you include the cost of the infinite number of governmental regulations, and the social costs caused by environmentalists perhaps in our own self-interest?

Answer: To the degree that legislation has already been passed and regulations are in effect, the cost of those affected technologies has already been internalized. That is, the price of a coal-fired boiler already includes the cost of meeting the Clean Air Act requirements. We were just looking at the costs as they actually existed in the marketplace in 1978 and that included everything that had been adopted. Some environmentalists would say it does not include a lot of things that should be there, and others might say it already includes too much, but we just took the market as it was. In fact, we did an interesting thing. We ran the numbers on replacement costs; we used the prices that might occur if we had a totally free market, and it just accelerated the result. We got a lot more efficiency; it went up to something like 44 percent instead of 33 percent, mostly at the expense of power generation.

Question: There are many institutional problems to cogeneration—as you mentioned, the Industrial Power Plant and Fuel Use Act, Clean Air Act—and many utilities are not interested unless they can control and dispatch cogeneration. Despite the fact that you do not want to talk in terms of barrels and kilowatt-hours, can you estimate how many barrels per day cogeneration could save?

Answer: No, I cannot.

Question: Or as a percent, some idea of how significant this could be?

Answer: Well, as I indicated, we found that about 43 percent of the electricity now being generated centrally would be displaced, and about two-thirds of that would be cogeneration. As a rough approximation, 29 percent of the present power generation could conceivably be satisfied at a lower cost by cogeneration. The part that attracts me the most about cogeneration, frankly, is that the utilities might do it. It is in their interest. You see, the utilities now are looking at a marginal cost of, say, eight cents a kilowatt-hour for putting in new power. They may be able to put in cogeneration at a cost, let us say, of four or five cents per kilowatt-hour. The utilities could invest in cogeneration technology as part of their system and include the cost in their rate base. The economics of that are much more attractive than getting the industrial user to compete with the utility. Furthermore, if they did cogeneration in a wholesale way, utilities could control and optimize the system in a way the industrial users never could do. (Our numbers assume that this is the way cogeneration would be operated, because that would be the least costly way of doing it.) The other way, utilities would want to protect their market share as did Consolidated Edison in New York.

Question: I like your optimism, but you indicated that the total cost of energy service to the consumer would not be any more in another decade than when—now, or somewhere between now and the next decade?

Answer: By the time the decade is over, if you look at the cost of heat, and not the cost of fuel, it will be about the same in real terms. Heat for buildings, for instance, is now costing us something like 28 percent more than it needs to. We have got a lot of cushion, so even if fuel prices rise in real terms faster than inflation generally, the ability to offset fuel prices with improved efficiency of the building, controls, and furnaces is so large that it can be offset such that the cost of heat in 1990 will be the same in real terms as it is today. I think the same thing is going to be true of other energy uses. The only place where it looks to me that the cost will be higher will be per mile in the automobile.

Question: If billions of dollars are going to be attracted to your least-cost energy opportunities, they will have to compete against other types of business investment. I am wondering if your studies took that into consideration—what rates of return result, and would they be sufficient to compete with other uses of capital?

Answer: Very good. That is probably the major uncertainty. Again, using the example of cogeneration, if the industrial user is paying the average price, not the marginal price, for electricity, he is immediately out of parity from the point of view of the utility. Furthermore, the typical industrial user has a higher cost of capital and certainly better investment opportunities than the utility.

My only way around that is to keep probing the opportunities for utilities to make the investments themselves as an alternative to new supply investments. And I do not know to what degree that will happen. My guess is that, by the 1990s, the power generation side of electricity will be deregulated. Then anybody would compete with the distribution company to provide the cheapest electricity possible. So it probably will not happen in conventional terms; it will happen through middle men.

Honeywell was my example of making the investment on behalf of the commercial-building-owner client. Honeywell would be selling a complete service; therefore, it would be in the company's interest to make the investment and Honeywell would do so with more confidence than the building owner. My understanding is that the institutional solution will be quite different. Different people will offer the service, and it will be in their interest as part of their product line to make the investment rather than in the user's interest to make the investment.

You may decide differently, but certainly when there is an opportunity around, somebody is going to find a way to make money with it. When the economics are there, an investor will make arrangements in such a way that a profit emerges. I do not know exactly what the mechanisms will be, but the examples I gave are indications.

13 What Is Conservation?

Walter J. Mead

Have you ever heard anybody speaking out against conservation? No, it is a motherhood term. Everybody is in favor of conservation. You are not saying a thing when you come out strongly in favor of conservation until you define what you mean by conservation. Daniel Yergin did not do that in his speech and does not do it in his book, *Energy Future*.[1] A naive view of conservation is implied in his work: *conservation* means use less. That is about what conservation means in Washington these days, and it is no theory at all.

Economists have a definition of conservation. It is only three words: *maximize present value*. The trouble is nobody knows what it means except businessmen, when they think about it. Maximize present value denotes use scarce resources over time in such a way so as to render the present value of those resources the greatest at some discount rate. That may or may not help you, but that is what conservation means economically: to rationally spread the use of resources over time.

But conservation also has a meaning at a given point in time, and it is simple: minimize your input of resources per unit of output. Everybody knows what that means. Or turn it around if you like: maximize output per unit of resources used. Either way, resource conservation occurs.

I suspect many conservationists would agree that that is a good definition. Minimize resource input per unit of output. It should sound familiar to businessmen because it is exactly the same as maximizing profit. The only difference is that in some circles the latter is bad and the former is good. Conservation is a good word; profit maximization is bad. Yet they are synonymous.

Any businessman who does not minimize his costs per unit of revenue is not in business long. Every businessman allocates resources over time in making an investment. He computes an internal rate of return, or, given an interest rate, he maximizes the excess of present revenues over costs. It is standard procedure in business. That is conservation. It has been going on for a long time, but the trouble with Yergin is, after suggesting that we decontrol oil as the first step, he then went on to urge conservation. His view of conservation is not to get government out of the business of making these decisions and let the market do it. His readers get the distinct feeling that he saw a very important role for government here — to force us to conserve.

Government-Enforced Conservation

After one decides against letting the market implement the conservation process, there are three choices. First, you can do it by imposing taxes to penalize one kind of activity. Second, you can grant subsidies to lead decision makers to do something the government wants. Third, you can impose regulations that say "thou shall not" under any conditions. But where did we ever get the idea that government could make those decisions for us better than we can make them for ourselves? Is government really that smart?

Further, suppose we decided that a given kind of energy program was ideal for the nation as a whole. We would approach Senator So-and-so with a petition that says, "Here is the way to go." The petition calls for either a tax, a subsidy, or a regulation, and the senator will introduce it because it has a lot of signatures on it. When the hearings start, along comes the Chamber of Commerce, the AFL-CIO, the Sierra Club, every group that has an economic interest in the proposal. They all make presentations. What comes out of that hearing is not at all what we put into it.

What comes out is what is politically acceptable, what Congress can vote for. Then come ten years of regulation, where legislation is put into effect, and regulation distorts it further. About ten years later, what we thought was a good idea is converted into something acceptable to the industry most regulated by it. What we thought was pursuing the general welfare in conservation or in alternative energy sources bears no relationship to conservation. And when you try to get rid of that regulation after discovering that is is counterproductive, major airline companies suggest that if the airlines are decontrolled, the people will suffer. It turns out the airline industry is the beneficiary of the regulation, not the people. The same will be true of any other area of regulation.

To believe that the government will solve our energy problems is to ignore history. Let me summarize the record of U.S. energy policy very quickly. The major tax policies over a half century are percentage depletion allowance and intangible drilling cost expensing—two big tax items. Now those are dear to the hearts of oil people. From an economic point of view, here is what they do. Any time you cut taxes for any group, it raises the after-tax rate of return in that industry, attracts capital which, over time, increases the output of the product (gasoline in this case), causing its price to be lower than it would be otherwise. After the initial impact of the tax, the after-tax rate of return becomes normal again, but the effect is too much capital in that industry and artificially low prices. The result is what Yergin talked about—big cars. That is the story of government tax policy for fifty years.

Consider that the old input quota system was very questionable. Why did we keep foreign oil out? Is not it obvious that this policy drains America first? Of course it is. Go back to the import quota hearings and it becomes abundantly clear why we did it. The coal industry did not want competition from residual fuel oil. The independent producers of oil in this country did not want competition from imports. The oil majors opposed it, of course. It was their oil that was to be excluded.

Government responded to the dominant political pressures brought to bear on it. It always has; it always will. We should not expect anything else; the same result occurs whether the dominant pressure is the coal industry, the oil industry, or environmentalists or consumer advocates.

Market Failures

When we talk about alternative energy sources, before we go down the road of government subsidy to coal liquefaction, coal gasification, and so forth, remember that what government does primarily is respond to a dominant interest group. The general welfare is a secondary consideration.

Economists have pointed out that in some instances the presence of "externalities" creates imperfect resource allocations. Externalities lead people to say, "We must correct for the market failure by having government intervene." They are forgetting the next problem. It is called political failure. We hand the problem to government and say, "Solve it," but the market in Congress is imperfect, too. It is the market for votes. That is what a congressman has to be concerned with; he has to get reelected. And is the primary concern general welfare? Of course not. It is getting elected. So we start with market imperfection and go down the road that breeds more imperfection; then we end up worse than we were before.

So, I am a Churchillian. Private enterprise and the free market is the worst system of allocating resources, except for the next best system, which is much worse.

Note

1. Roger Stobaugh and Daniel Yergin, eds., *Energy Future: The Report of the Harvard Business School Energy Project* (New York: Random House, 1979).

14 Impacts of Alternative Energy Resources

Laurence I. Moss

Alternative energy resources and their social/economic and environmental impacts are especially important today. *Alternative* here is defined as everything other than oil—in other words, natural gas, coal, coal-derived synfuels, oil shale, nuclear, solar, and so forth. Several authorities claim that our past energy policies have failed, and we have to try something different. But I have somewhat different observations based on some of the energy policies of the last few years and their results.

One policy has been to subsidize oil imports through the entitlements program and foreign tax credits. The result is that we import more oil. Another policy has been to subsidize small refiners. The result is that sixty-five inefficient small refineries blossomed forth in the land. Another policy has been to hold prices of domestic oil, natural gas, and electricity below marginal or replacement cost levels. The result is, for oil and natural gas, domestic production dropped. For all of these policies, economically justified investments in improved end-use efficiency and decentralized supplies are not made.

Another policy we have had is to treat air and water as free goods, obliging us to issue what truly are licenses to pollute. There is no incentive at all in the state implementation plan to perform better than minimum allowable emissions, even if it is economically justifiable. And the result has been that progress in pollution abatement is exceedingly difficult. Overall emissions of sulfur dioxide, and especially nitrogen oxides, are projected to increase, even with the best available control technology and other regulations in force. Regional air pollution problems are exacerbated.

All of the above difficulties and more conceal the true relative costs of available alternatives in supplying end-use demands for goods and services. These are the end-use demands to which Roger Sant refers. And we end up doing things, therefore, in ways that are more costly. We use a more expensive mix of resources to get a particular demand satisfied; therefore, inflation roars ahead. Price controls on energy do not put a lid on inflation; they exacerbate inflation.

My conclusion from this litany is that economic incentives and disincentives as expressed primarily through prices have been remarkably effective in achieving an obvious result. A corollary conclusion is that an extensive regulatory apparatus is usually ineffective in the face of contrary economic incentives. So the failure of past policy has been with respect to the illusion of what that policy was, rather than to its reality.

Pricing Decontrol

If we want to reduce imports, avoid waste in the allocation of scarce resources, and move more quickly in achieving our environmental quality goals, we have to set the right prices. With the correct prices, we have every reason to expect success. This means, for natural gas and oil, decontrol of prices. For electricity it means more use of incremental or marginal cost considerations in designing rate structures, probably best done within traditional revenue constraints so as not to overcollect revenue by monopoly utilities. I think there are ways this can be done—not perfect, but much better than those we employ now.

For air and water, the right pricing means to experiment with and levy emission charges and effluent fees to get away from treating those resources as free goods for which there is no cost. They are scarce social goods for which charges should be collected. For synfuels it means no subsidy for commercialization because that disguises the real costs of the marginal energy supply.

Now some would say that reasonable prices would allow those companies and individuals who have more resources to avoid any changes. If you are wealthy, you just pay and do what you were doing before. But why would they do that? Does General Motors use more steel in its automobiles because it can afford to do so because it has a strong competitive position? Of course not. It seeks to minimize costs in supplying various end-use demands and services.

As a matter of fact, however, the people who are better off often have more choices. They have better access to capital; in the case of an industrial organization, they usually have a better research department. They know more about the alternatives than people who are less well off. If there is any problem, it is in making sure that capital and information are similarly available for those who are not in as good a position, rather than worrying about what people who are in a very good position will do.

The present policies that I have listed, which have been so effective in rewarding waste and pollution, were not created in a vacuum. Why were they ever considered? Why, when every president since President Nixon has talked about the need to cut oil imports, have we subsidized such imports? Why, when we have talked about the importance of conservation, have we held down energy prices that conceal the true cost of replacement supplies?

At this point, a nice word rears its ugly head. The word is *equity*. Who can be against a nice word like that? Everybody's in favor of equity, but what does it mean? In energy policy, it means maintaining the status quo. The status quo to which the equity advocate refers can be so narrow and justified it will not cause a relative worsening of the position of people of low income, or it can be so broad and unjustified it will maintain the status quo of different regions of the country, or producers vis-a-vis consumers, or maintain historical advantages or historical trading relationships. For example, some equity advocates want to maintain the status quo of refiners who have historically relied on imported oil and not put them at a competitive disadvantage as relative prices change between world and domestic oil.

In short, equity has become a code word for a plethora of efforts to insulate economic decision makers from the realities of the marketplace. Let us not insist that energy policy carry the burden of our compassion toward those of low income who could be helped more effectively through emergency payments, capital subsidies (for example, of insulation) or income transfers. If energy policy is asked to carry that burden, it will not solve the other problems we have been talking about.

Well, this leaves us with all those bureaucrats in Washington. What are they going to do? What possible role can we envisage for the people whose services will not be needed to allocate energy supplies and control prices? I propose that we put them in the business of regulating the use of the word *equity*.

Energy Market Failures

More seriously, what is the proper role of government in energy policy? I would say it is to correct and compensate for what are truly market failures. In a question to Congressman Stockman I referred to the national security costs of large-scale reliance on imported oil. And I think he quite correctly pointed out that it should be internalized through a fee on imported oil that could then be used to pay for a large stockpile to help buffer the effects of any cutoff. I agree with that; I think that he has perhaps underestimated what the magnitude of the fee should be. It should include not only the maintenance costs of the stockpile, but also the effect of that stockpiled oil on world oil prices. He used a figure of 2 to 3 billion barrels in stockpile over the next two to three years, which is about 3 million barrels a day. It is a sizable amount of oil, and our bidding for it in competition with other buyers will have the effect of raising world oil prices. The fee on imported oil should reflect that. So it is more than a few cents or a dollar. It is probably many dollars.

The second market failure has to do with environmental pollution, which is an externality. I may be concerned about the air I breathe or the air I have to look through if I want to see the mountains, but I cannot go into any market and buy a few cubic miles of clean air wherever I am. I have to work through a political decision-making process to see whether I can get my values to be considered in that decision.

Here I think we need a mix of price (that is, the emission charges and effluent fees that I mentioned) and regulatory strategies, with more emphasis on the price strategies than we have had up to now. We should create a marketplace for what is indeed a scarce public good; namely, the limited capacity of the air and water to take pollution to the levels that are socially acceptable.

The third market failure is probably in the area of information. I think the government can intervene to require mandatory labeling and full disclosure on the energy and dollar costs that are likely to be derived from various choices of appliances, dwelling units, and so forth.

The fourth market failure has to do with areas where clearly natural monopolies exist, such as in the transmission and distribution of electricity. It would not be economical to have two or three or four electrical transmission and distribution companies serving the same area. I tend to agree, however, with Roger Sant that there is not obviously a natural monopoly in electrical generation, any more than a natural monopoly exists in providing telephones that you plug into the American Telephone and Telegraph system (see chapter 12).

Nevertheless, where you have natural monopolies, regulation of prices is required by government, but it should be done with more regard for having these prices reflect the marginal costs in those parts of the rate structure where users will save or lose from their investment decisions. So you should be able to benefit not in the customer charges, the amount you pay each month just to be hooked into the system, but more on the *tail blocks*, the accessories and options.

There is another market failure, I think, in support for research and development. Economists point out that individual entrepreneurs, since they cannot recapture all of the benefit of their research yield, will tend to invest less than the socially optimum amount in research. The government has an important role to play here and to some extent in product demonstration (short of commercialization) because a comprehensive analysis of all factors, economical as well as technical, gets to the question of a development's true costs.

Energy Policies

We have heard about the competition between hard versus soft technologies, and centralized versus decentralized installations. The important principle here is to compare all costs of the alternatives and select those alternatives that are lower in cost in preference to those that are higher in cost. The matter of centralization or decentralization in itself should not be paramount.

Note, however, that decentralized technologies have a built-in advantage that a centralized technology lacks. That is the nature of decentralization—visible in the community, flexible to its needs, always available for use. Whatever residual external impacts arise will be brought home closer to the user because they will occur right where the user is. And that is an advantage to be considered, although it is not necessarily a determining factor. Other costs have to be considered as well.

On the question of whether existing environmental standards are excessive or inadequate, I will defend every one of the existing standards. By and large, they are reasonably well-conceived, considering all the values involved. I believe we should have greater concern over regional air pollution impacts, which are not now directly addressed in laws and regulations: acid precipitation, regional impairment of visibility, and the production—long after emission in fine particle form by atmospheric conversion—of sulfur oxides and nitrogen oxides and of acid sulfates and nitrates. Other effects of air pollution and potential health need much more attention.

In terms of regulatory strategy, we ought to shift more than we have in the direction of looking at regional emissions or total emissions of some of these key pollutants and not have such a fixation on the ground-level concentration of presently regulated pollutants in the immediate vicinity of the emitters. Of course, we should not allow local levels to increase unnecessarily or without limit, but handling that problem is not addressing the full problem, or even perhaps the most important problem.

Cost/Benefit Analyses

On the question of cost/benefit analyses, which industry always calls for, they ask, "Are these regulations cost-justified?" We have to consider how such an analysis should be done. The analyst can go only so far in comparing costs and benefits of proposed regulations. For example, consider the effect of acid precipitation on the fish life in the Adirondack lakes. There are about a hundred lakes in New York State's Adirondack Mountains, with lightly buffered soils around them, that have been rendered sterile for fish life because of acid precipitation. The analyst can calculate the pounds of fish that would have been caught in those lakes and figure that fish meat is worth $1.50 per pound and then come up with what probably turns out to be a pretty small cost. But that does not begin to touch the depth of concern that many people legitimately have for man's drastic intervention with natural ecosystems.

Take the case of impairment of regional visibility. You can calculate the small dollar amount that that might have on delaying air traffic when it gets really bad, but again, you would not begin to touch the concerns of most people, in terms of aesthetics in the western states—being able to see the mountains and the vivid colors of the landscape. Now how do you weigh these factors in the cost/benefit analysis? There is no perfect way. And when we talk about cost/benefit analysis, we have to consider the full political process where intangibles are weighed, and not just the analytical part of it.

Eric Zausner believes we need to know what the costs of synfuels are in order to put a lid on the cost of oil in the world market (see chapter 11). I do not think that argument stands up to scrutiny. First of all, if he is right and the costs might range to $200 a barrel, I am not sure we want to know what the lid is. If the lid actually were $200 a barrel, would we want to reveal it, thereby encouraging producers of conventional fuels to raise their price to that level?

But, in fact, we do have a fairly good idea of the cost now, within 10 to 20 percent, not counting general rates of inflation, for first-generation plants like gasification plants. Second-generation plants will probably be within 20 to 30 percent of the costs of those of the first generation. A lid, to be effective, must comprise existing, not potential, capacity of 5 to 10 million barrels a day; otherwise, it will not be taken seriously. And that is not going to happen within the next twenty or twenty-five years.

With regard to the environmental barriers that might exist, a properly designed synfuels plant should have less impact than conventional coal combustion. So let synfuels commercialization occur when the market is ready.

Despite our best efforts—I would say our worst efforts—to conceal the real costs, oil prices have increased and changes in energy use have begun. But as the government role in economic regulation diminishes, we need to make sure that future government participation is properly defined and that effective implementing mechanisms are selected to keep the government properly involved in the areas where market failures would otherwise occur.

15 A Partnership for Alternative Energy Development

Timothy E. Wirth

There is no reason for us in the country or in the Congress to be hesitant about whether environmental policies over the last ten years have been effective and have been good for the country. We should be very proud about the fact that we have made some very significant progress. Look at the automobile market in this country. We are now embarked on a second generation of technology in automobile emissions. Clean air and health standards have become very important products for all Americans. The Cuyahoga River is no longer on fire. The question of waste disposal of toxic substances, PCB and so on, is now in front of all Americans.

Clearly, there have been some problems in overzealous activities and harassing regulations. But keeping in mind the long-term goal, I think we have nothing to be apologetic about but rather have many very proud accomplishments behind us. And it is up to all of us to make sure that we maintain those accomplishments and learn from the mistakes of the past in a better honing of the coalition concerned about the environment.

I agree with Dr. Mead about the need for government decontrol, where we are all in agreement (see chapter 13). I was the floor leader of the vote for decontrol in the House in September 1979, and I think that that vote will go down as the most significant step taken by the House of Representatives in the Ninety-sixth Congress. But I also disagree with Dr. Mead, in three areas in particular. First, that government responds to pressures and people in the society. That is what government is meant to do in large part. Government's challenge is to respond to felt needs in groups within the society and to orchestrate that in a very complicated pluralistic society of 220 million people and come out with some direction. That response is one of the strong parts of this democratic society.

My second disagreement is that reelection is a political market mutually exclusive to the general welfare. Again, I would take great issue with that; within a society of many diverse interests, a lot of specific geographic, economic, and ideological differences are felt in that political marketplace. But to assume that public interest gets lost in the face of all those interests being played out does not credit the dynamics and the talent that exists in the political process and the immense promise that we have in that process.

Finally, that we can somehow draw a line between the government and the market; that there is somehow a clear division or a plurality or a barrier between the two is absolutely unrealistic.

Energy Partnerships

Oil decontrol, with the price of energy going up very sharply, leaves a large number of people in this society in an absolutely desperate situation, the poor and the elderly in particular. I can tell you that as an operating politician dealing with individuals who simply cannot pay their fuel bills. The market is not going to take care of those people. With rising prices, part of which results from decontrol and most of which results from someplace else, we have a mutual obligation to make sure these individuals are not forced to make the classic choice between buying food or buying fuel.

We have another obligation we are willing to accept, and that is part of the partnership we talk about between the private sector and the public sector. With prices going up, taxes for the private sector rise, and the government allocates its income to cover rising administrative costs.

Some other problems that result from our energy crisis cannot be solved by the private sector, and partnership with government is again needed. In my own state of Colorado, 80 percent of our known oil shale reserves exist. Let us assume, as did some of the early administration documents, that somehow we could reach a million-barrel-a-day shale-oil production by the mid-1990s. To do that, and assuming both in situ and surface retort processes, we would have, within a 100-mile radius in the Piceance Basin in Colorado, a recovery operation equivalent to all of the coal mining that is going on in the United States today. In that 100-mile-radius area there are today eight towns with a total population of 14,500 people.

An Energy Industry

Best estimates are that to reach one million barrels a day, there would be a population increase of 200,000 people. This would involve community-service investments of at least $1 billion in funding up front, not including housing and transportation, and an investment for the processes that develop a community of some $7,000 per person in today's dollars. Who is going to pay for those costs? That is a very significant problem we face in this country. Are we going to ask the citizens of the state of Colorado to defray that large cost? You can scale it down from a million barrels a day to 200,000 barrels a day, or 100,000 barrels a day, yet there are some significant costs that simply are not going to come in from tax revenues until later. Who is going to make that front-end investment?

Again, it seems to me we are looking at a partnership. If we are going to embark on developing synthetic fuels, the industry handles the synthetic fuels technology; the government must handle all of those other impacts that are necessary for the people who are going to live there.

Consider the problem of water: 73 percent of the rainfall in the United States occurs east of the Mississippi River; 14 percent occurs in the Pacific Northwest; and 13 percent occurs in the rest of the country. For a population explosion in Colorado that creates a set of problems and a set of allocations. Which should we leave to the private sector? Or is some kind of joint decision to be made? It seems to me that this is one of the most severe public policy decisions. What do we do in allocating that very scarce resource among the national requirements for energy development, tourism, agriculture, towns, and all of the other competing needs? Who is going to make that decision? Does it get made in the marketplace? The highest bidder can take that water, which is possible under Colorado water law; or are we going to have some other framework in which we make that decision?

Those are some of the considerations. I would say quite strongly that, rather than attempting to develop some kind of a dividing line between the government and industry, a more realistic and productive approach would be to create a partnership between the two. That partnership will be absolutely essential if we are going to embark upon alternative fuels.

We can also get into the specifics of partnerships in solar energy, conservation, coal gasification, coal liquefaction, oil shale, and others; but the hallmark, it seems to me, has got to be a creative partnership and a willingness by both the industry side and government to recognize this two-way street. Just as industry asks government to understand its economic and commercial problems, we have the right to ask industry to understand government's concerns for people's welfare and safety. Only in that kind of understanding will we be able to move creatively without the sort of confrontations that have existed in the past.

Questions and Answers to Part V

Question: Congressman Wirth, do you think there is an optimistic program wherein we can educate consumers and voters so that politicians are not pressured to make irresponsible regulations or irresponsible statements in public?

Answer: Clearly there is a possibility of getting a lot of education across to people, but you do not get it accomplished with vague abstractions. Would not it be nice if somehow we had a national leader saying, "This is what a barrel of oil looks like; we use 17 million of these every day. Now half of these come from the Middle East, and the other half come from domestic production, and in the Middle East this is where those sources come from." And then point to a map and say, "This is how wide the straits are, and anybody could close down those straits with the use of modern weaponry. The crisis is real."

It is very difficult when you have forty-five seconds on evening news—and that is where most people get their news. It's very difficult to get that message across to people. It is a long and painful process, but it is also a process that involves every single one of us as well. You have to keep hammering away and hammering away. Nothing happens quickly in terms of the change of attitudes.

Question: One of the most outstanding jobs in communication and moving the public mind has been done within the environmental movement.

Answer: (Laurence Moss) We're all engaged, at least in part, in the business of public education. Trying to explain our positions, our values, why we think certain things are important to do, why certain values should be maintained—this is all hard work. I do not know that the environmentalists do such a perfect job of it. We make a lot of mistakes; we have some successes.

I have been engaged over the last few years in the National Coal Policy Project, in which we bring together people from both the environmental and the industrial community. Together we explore areas of possible agreement where neither of our respective values would be compromised. And we think we have been quite successful identifying some important policy areas where we can agree. Because when two or more protagonists or opponents get together, study an issue, and then come out with a recommendation on which they agree, people tend to sit up and pay more notice—at least the policymakers do—than when it is just one group or another making public pronouncements. So I hope that that will be more of a model for the future on impacting the public process and educating people on the potential for moving ahead.

Question: We appreciate the need for moving forward, expanding programs, getting government and industry walking side-by-side. But I have not heard any mention of where the money is going to come from. In the last ten years at least, one side is waiting for the other because of over-regulation or underinvestment or whatever it might be. But we are all at the same starting line waiting for the gun to go off. And we are all going to run for the same pile of dollars at the same time, and somebody is going to come up short. Now is government going to continue to compete with industry for dollars, and is industry going to program its expenditures over a logical period of time so that we get the job done? I do not see where the capital comes from.

Answer: (Laurence Moss) One of the concerns I had when I said the government should not be in the business of subsidizing synfuels, which may turn out to be a high-cost option, is that in doing so it competes for capital with the private sector in ways that raise the cost of capital for everyone else. Now having said that, I do think it is necessary to increase the incentive for capital formation, even at the expense of current consumption. And a lot of proposals made for faster tax write-offs, possibly investment tax credits, and other ways to stimulate savings and investment make a lot of sense.

Answer: (Walter Mead) I would strongly object to a partnership between government and industry in developing future energy sources. I think that we have got a disaster brewing in Washington right now in transferring $227 billion over eleven years in the windfall profits tax. What you are doing is taking $227 billion over eleven years out of one decision-making structure, which is profit making—profiteering, if you want to use a bad word. It is based on costs and revenues and internal rates of return; it's conservation. You are turning the money over to government where those are not the relevant decision-making factors.

Government is going to distribute some to the poor; we are also going to stimulate alternative energy sources where rate of return to the public is a secondary factor. We all lose because government's claim on resources of $227 billion is going to be transferred and resources are going to be allocated in a way which will reduce our standard of living. Output per unit of input—that determines our standard of living.

I do not want such a partnership one bit. I would rather say to the industry, "You guys make an investment when you consider the rate of return to be attractive; and if you don't consider it attractive, don't make it." And I will tell you what that will mean. No oil company or coal company will go into coal liquefaction. We should not—it is a loser. No company should make alcohol for gasoline. It costs about $1.65 a gallon to do it. Why would anybody in his right mind do that when you can buy alcohol in Western European refineries for ninety-five cents per gallon (wholesale tax included). But we are taking that direction because government subsidies make it profitable to go that way.

Answer: (Congressman Wirth) I find it interesting that many of the people with whom we worked on the package of decontrol and the windfall profits tax and who, early in 1979 (pre-decontrol), were strong advocates of the windfall profits tax, are now, after decontrol has gone into effect, arguing about how evil the windfall profits tax is. It does not seem to me that you can have it both ways, and maybe we made a tactical error in not combining the two.

On the question of how much money there is around, the federal government is on an absolutely unsustainable course in terms of this year and the next five to ten years. That percentage of the federal budget which is so-called uncontrollable is now up to 76.6 percent. It is very clear that we must change strategies and demand the input and involvement of all kinds of parties. This is assuming a nonpartisan focus in Congress. We have a new process working in the Budget Committee that, in fact, grew out of a breakfast meeting among three of us: Dick Gebhardt, Democrat from Missouri, David Stockman, and I. It is a very exciting opportunity, but we are not going to be able to change that budgetary course to have an impact on ultimate capital availability in the country until we get the kind of broad national support for belt tightening.

Answer: (Laurence Moss) The scarcity of capital puts a premium on the kind of strategy that Roger Sant advocates, a least-cost strategy. We don't want to squander the limited resources that we have.

Answer: (Edward Myers) Just to bring into focus where the money comes from: today, there are solar electric plants, wind plants, and geothermal plants being built in Southern California, and the money is coming from the shareholders of the public utilities. A large amount of the money funding for the solar plant is coming from the Department of Energy to demonstrate the first solar-generating plant in the world of major size connected to a utility system.

As far as taking care of the poor people is concerned, in California the regulated utilities, both gas and electric, have a lifeline rate. The nonlifeline users pay for the lifeline subsidy, which runs at the present time about 25 percent below the cost of production. Unfortunately, it does not apply to just the needy or the seniors but to every residential customer in the State of California. The result has been that residential rates have gone up 19 percent in the last four years, and commercial and industrial rates have gone up as much as 70 percent. So if you want to know where the capital's coming from, it is going to come from all of us as individuals, either through rates, taxes, or some other way.

Question: Congressman Wirth, you alluded to Colorado's shale oil potential and the development of communities in the surrounding areas. Did you mean local communities developing the sewage systems and the power lines in the different cities and letting private enterprise develop the housing and infrastructure? What kind of plan did you have in mind to develop these cities in conjunction with production of up to one million barrels per day of shale oil?

Answer: We have two different models. One is the model we see in Rock Springs (Colorado) or in the Powder River Basin in Wyoming. This is a model of laissez-faire, I think, which avoids making the investment at the front end in the housing. That has to be a public investment. There is no market out there until the mining process gets going and the tax revenues come in two or three years down the line. If you look at the impact this has had on employment in Rock Springs, on the alcoholism rate, on the absenteeism rate, the social cost of people living in trailer camps with no community institutions, bad school systems, and having to drive as far as Salt Lake City to find a doctor, the social cost is immense.

We have come to understand that in energy development in the Rocky Mountain region, rather than waiting, the front-end investment model is the one that has to be followed. Then the question becomes: Where is the money going to come from for that front-end investment? Those of us in the State of Colorado think that the citizens of the state do not have the funds; therefore, front-end investment is either going to have to be some kind of bonding operation from the private sector or come directly from the government itself. Maybe some combination of the two is possible.

Answer: (Walter Mead) I really do not think the government ought to solve our social problems for us. If people want to live in trailers for two years, why do you want to settle that problem for us?

Answer: (Congressman Wirth) You cannot tell me that a family of four wants to live in a trailer. You cannot tell me that they want to drink unclear water. You can't tell me that they want to drive 300 miles to Salt Lake City to get a doctor. Now to say that the market somehow is going to become an enterprise that is in the business of providing social services to get business into businesses with which it should not be and doesn't want to be involved. It is government's job to do that and, hopefully, to do it well.

Answer: (Walter Mead) Providing housing?

Answer: (Congressman Wirth) Absolutely. To provide housing if it is not there or to require that housing be developed there.

**Part VI
Summary**

16 Changes in U.S. Economy

Arthur B. Laffer

When you look at the energy industry and at energy problems in the United States, they reflect a microcosmic caricature of the entire set of problems facing the United States and perhaps the Western-world economies as well. If you look at the U.S. economy, you will see the analogies here. The economic patterns are quite the same, and this is so not only in the results but also in the types of solutions that have been proffered to the energy industry.

We in academia work out models quite carefully, based on assumptions and academic and theoretical types of input. The basic inputs that we employ in the academic world are very different from practical ways of looking at problems. The underlying assumption used, for example, is that people do not work to pay taxes. We think that businesses do not locate their plant facilities as a matter of social conscience; we expect that businesses basically locate their plant facilities to make an after-tax rate of return on their investment.

Further, we assume that people do not hold money to go bankrupt. People respond to incentives, and, when you change incentives, people change their behavior. People allocate their time according to the rates of return associated with each and every activity; likewise, they allocate their capital according to the net after-tax rates of return on this capital. And they likewise allocate their money balance holdings by the degree of depreciation of the individual money.

The Last Fifteen Years

Over the last fifteen years, a new *demand* strategy or sort of contractionist perception of the United States and the world has had an important influence on public policy. Tax rates, especially marginal tax rates, have increased in the United States by enormous amounts. Many of these increases affected the energy industry. In the mid-1950s the focus was on tariffs and oil import quotas. More recently, oil rationing has been tried. In the U.S. economy we have practiced allocation by fiat as well as by the energy industry. Finally, we have devalued the currency in the United States.

Let me take you back in a journey to the year 1965 and what the U.S. economy looked like prior to these infusions of demand side/contractionist economic policies. In that year, the unemployment rate was less than 4 percent; the inflation rate was 1.5 percent (that was when they measured it per year, not per month, the way they do now). The Consumer Price Index for February 1980 increased 1.4 percent. The wholesale price index for that month was up 1.7 percent. That was greater than for the entire year of 1965. In 1965, the federal budget was in surplus. In 1965, the prime interest rate was 4.5 percent. In February 1980, the prime was 16.75 percent.

In 1965, the United States had just experienced five straight years of rapid growth, where our real GNP increased on the average about 5.5 percent per year. The federal budget went from a deficit to a surplus. In the year 1965 the Dow Jones Industrial Average, in dollar terms, averaged 910 for the year. In February 1980, it was in the neighborhood of 970. If the Dow figures of 1965 were put with those prices, they would total about 2300. This gives a picture of what has happened.

In 1962 and 1964, the United States cut taxes, and cut them a lot. During the Kennedy administration, the personal income tax was reduced for everyone by about 30 percent, cutting the tax rates the most on the upper income groups. Corporate taxes were cut. The tax rate on corporations was 52 percent prior to Kennedy's coming into office. The Kennedy tax bills then reduced it to 48 percent. He had tried to lower it to 46 percent, but Congress deemed it irresponsible. Tax lives for depreciation purposes were reduced in that administration, again cutting the tax rates on capital, as well as enacting the investment tax credit for the first time in U.S. history. They also cut taxes on traded products, called the Kennedy Round Tariff Negotiation.

From the late 1960s on, we have switched our policies, and you can see the results. I like to juxtapose the Kennedy administration period with our perceptions of the Kennedy and subsequent administrations. The Kennedy administration cut federal spending as a share of GNP by almost one full percent. Do your perceptions include the fact that the federal budget went from a deficit of almost $4 billion to a surplus of about a half a billion in 1965? Inflation rates were controlled. The stock market climbed sharply.

President Nixon came into office in 1969. The demand policies, the contractionist policies, of the past decade began during the first year of his administration. The capital gains tax was doubled. Then we had a little inflation pushing people into higher tax brackets, reducing their incentives, and raising the effective rates of taxation on corporate-held capital, causing a contraction there at least.

In 1971 Nixon put on probably the most severe wage and price controls the country has ever seen. He added a 10 percent surcharge across the board. We had the sharpest increase in social spending as a share of GNP of any administration ever in U.S. history. We went from a federal budget surplus of $8 billion in 1969 to a deficit of about $70 billion by 1975. Inflation during that period averaged 7 percent per annum; in fact, in 1974 we hit the magical 1 percent per month mark. By 1975, unemployment was almost 8 percent, compared to about 3.5 percent in 1969. Real GNP grew on an average of about 2.5 percent per annum.

When you look at the types of incentives here—the oil import quotas, the excess profits tax, the wellhead control prices, the allocation problems, the underdepreciation, the depletion allowance—you will see that all these intervention mechanisms treat the system as though there were no incentive effects at all. I think there have been disastrous results in the U.S. economy.

It may be worth having a little less output and more inflation, if we make our system fairer. Taking excess profits and giving them to the people may make the poor a little better off and may make some of the wealthy a little bit worse off—in fact, so much worse off that really their net income is lower. Nevertheless, we do make the poor better off. It is the notion of redistributionist economics, which is an essential part of U.S. policies, especially during the past fifteen years. This is sharply different from Kennedy, who basically said a rising tide raises all boats and that any man who tries to benefit by taking from another man makes us all worse off.

Robin Hood Revisited

The notion of redistribution was probably the first economics lesson in the Anglo-Saxon world. It is our worst lesson in economics in any world. It comes from that fourteenth-century ballad of a young knave from Yorkshire named Robin Hood. Basically the Robin Hood notion entirely underlies our policies: you make the poor a little better off; you make the rich a little bit worse off. In every field other than economics, this story makes eminent sense. But once you get into economics, it does not make sense anymore.

I will retell the story of Robin Hood, apply it to today, and then describe what it implies about incentives today. Robin Hood would wake up in the morning in Knottingham, and he would don his light-green leisure suit. And he would wait by a transforest throughway, and as a wealthy merchant would come by, Robin would take everything the guy had. He would let him run naked out of the forest.

Another fellow would come by, this one was just rich. Robin would take a lot, but would leave him a little bit. Now if a tradesman came by who was only prosperous, Robin would again take proportionately less. If Robin found a guy who was just barely making it, Robin would take only a token amount.

What Robin Hood did was steal from the rich, but they had so much, they could afford it—like the oil companies, like individuals in the higher income tax brackets. At the end of the day, Robin would load up his contraband and he would go zipping back to Knottingham. If he found some guy walking the street who had nothing, just down and out, Robin Hood would give him a trunkful. And if he found an ordinary citizen passing by, doing all right, Robin Hood (just to show he was on the job and was a good guy) would give him a little token. You may remember this in the United States—President Ford's $50 per capita rebate.

What Robin Hood did was steal from the rich and give to the poor, and the story insisted that somehow he made the rich less well off, but it was worth it because, frankly, he made the poor better off. But let me introduce incentives into the story.

Imagine for a moment that you are a Knottingham merchant in those ancient days. How long would it take you to learn not to go through the forest? People do not like to be waylaid by Robin Hood. People do not like to pay taxes. They hire accountants and lawyers; they get Bermuda tax shelters and other sorts of tax dodges. People avoid. Well, in the old Knottingham days, what would you expect of these merchants trying to trade with the neighboring villages? They took the circuitous route around the forest. That cost a lot of money. If they did go through the forest they hired armed guards to protect them from Robin Hood. That cost a lot, too.

Now, if it cost them a lot more to do business with the neighboring villages, did the merchants sell their goods at higher or lower prices? Obviously they sold to the rich and poor alike, at higher prices. Now Robin Hood, hiding there in the forest deep, finds that the only merchants who come by are so heavily armed he cannot take anything from them. Robin comes back to Knottingham empty handed, leaving the poor now to face the tradesmen's higher prices imposed on the economic system. By taxing the rich and giving to the poor, all Robin Hood has really done is to make the poor literally worse off.

You can see the story in different forms. Capital and labor and rich and poor are not economic enemies in the system. You do not make the poor better off by taxing the rich. Symmetrically, you do not make the rich better off by taxing the poor. Capital and labor work hand-in-hand; rich and poor work hand-in-hand. It is Kennedy's rising tide that raises all. There is virtually no association whatsoever between the incidence of the tax structure and the burden of that tax structure; the person on whom you place a tax does not necessarily bear the burden of that tax. As often as not, the tax burden ends up somewhere else, as you can see by the results that New York City or Great Britain have had in eliminating poverty by redistributionist economic policies. The one major benefit in California since the passage of Proposition 13 is the enormous reduction in the unemployment rate. Unfortunately, we have not improved the distribution of income in the United States; we have made the poor poorer.

17 Impact of the Market Pricing System

Thornton F. Bradshaw

I do believe that we in the United States, as a country, are coming together on energy. In a larger sense, the people of the United States are coming together. We are getting over our malaise of the 1970s and 1960s. We have left Watergate and Vietnam far enough behind us so that now we are coming together with a sense of shared values that can hold our society together once more. This is being reflected not only in our approach to foreign affairs and our democracy, but also in terms of our approach to this energy problem.

Energy Myths

In the past we have lived on myths so far as energy is concerned. Specifically, two myths. One myth was that energy was unlimited, that over the horizon in the Middle East were oil fields that would continue to pour forth their oil to the United States forever. We also lived on the myth of cheap energy, a myth that was enhanced because Congress decreed the people of the United States deserved prices lower than the people of the rest of the world. And therefore, for the past ten years, energy in the United States indeed has been cheap by world standards.

We built two policies on these energy myths, and both were successful. Policy number one was to use more foreign oil. In 1970 we used about 3.5 million barrels a day of oil from foreign sources at a cost of about $3 billion, and by the end of the decade, we used about 8 million barrels a day from foreign sources at a cost of about $80 billion. How successful can a policy be, if that indeed was the policy?

The second policy based on myth was to break OPEC. If we did believe energy truly was cheap, the only thing in the way of cheap energy from abroad was the existence of this economic cartel. "They" made prices high when the price in reality was low, because energy was indeed cheap. Therefore, our policy was to destroy the cartel, and once again we were successful.

We were not successful in the usual sense. In the usual sense, a cartel tends to fall apart because one of its members does not feel it is getting enough; therefore, it lowers the price in order to sell more product, to get more income. Then someone else undercuts, and the cartel falls apart. That is not the way it happened. The cartel appeared to fall apart in 1979 because members simply could not hold meetings fast enough to keep up with the market price. And the final meeting in Venezuela, in December, fell apart in a shambles because the real price of energy, the world market price, was rising so fast there was no way the members of the cartel could keep up with it.

So the United States had two policies based on myth. Both were successful; both had catastrophic results for us and the rest of the world. The first result was that United States oil production dropped. Production had topped in 1970, and from that point in time it began to run down at an ever-increasing rate. It declined for reasons that are well known: a lack of incentive to go out and drill expensive oil. Why would you go out and drill for more expensive oil if oil in reality was cheap? That was the myth, and therefore there was not the incentive under controlled prices to explore for the expensive oil, all that is left in the United States. And so, by the end of the decade, we were losing production at the rate of 500,000 barrels a day, and on a base of 10 million barrels a day, that is a severe loss indeed.

The second result of this misguided set of policies was that we pushed the oil-producing nations too hard. We pushed them beyond their capacity to absorb their national earnings. Each one of these nations, in the Middle East particularly, has one chance at emerging from an almost medieval kind of economy and society into the modern world. And that chance depends on the wise use of its oil resources. Iran provided a rather severe lesson. One of the causes of the revolution in Iran was a too rapid industrialization of a society unprepared to absorb that kind of industrialization. You could see the contrasts in the streets of Teheran.

That lesson has not been lost on Saudi Arabia or any of the other nations of the Middle East. Some of the oil-producing nations elsewhere did not need that kind of lesson, as a matter of fact. Norway decided long before the Iranian revolution that it was going to produce oil at a rate that was good for Norwegian economy and society—not at the rate the West demanded, nor that which the developed nations of the world demanded.

The third impact of this set of U.S. policies was that we pushed the Third World to the wall. The Third World uses energy to live, produce crops, transport those crops, and fuel basic industries. When energy fails them, it is not a question of missing the beach that weekend; people starve. Energy is the largest import to most of these Third World nations. It accounts for about one-half of the total foreign exchange of India and as an extreme example perhaps, it accounts for the total foreign exchange of the Dominican Republic. The impact of any kind of price rise on the Third World can be devastating. Our policies contributed to these price rises.

The fourth and final impact is the impact on our own dollar. The fact that the United States pays $80 billion for imports has had a very large impact on the dollar and has brought a large strain on the international banking system. There are very severe questions in the minds of bankers as to whether the international banking system can handle the increased flow of funds from developed nations to the developing oil-producing nations.

Administration Problems

All of these things add up to the fact that President Carter inherited a mess in 1977 when he became president. And to his everlasting credit, he recognized the basics of the problem and recognized them almost immediately. And they are that energy is essential to the economic growth of the United States, energy is no longer cheap, and we have begun to run out of time. Now those are the essentials, and most of us have recognized them for some time, but this was the first time a president of the United States had apparently recognized them and acted on them. In May of 1978, President Carter, using his own authority and not that of the Congress—going to Congress would have been futile at that time—set forth a program for the decontrol of U.S. oil prices so they would reach the world-market levels by 1981. This was an absolutely essential action. It was a brave action because the cheap energy lobby is the largest lobby in the United States.

President Carter could have stopped with decontrolling oil prices and let the market price system, the hidden hand of capitalism, take over. Market pricing, then, would provide the incentive to increase the supply. It would provide the disincentive for overuse of energy. It would provide an appropriate allocation of resources to the energy industry and, after a period of time, all would be well.

This would not have been possible. It in no way should be interpreted as any lack on my part of faith in the enterprise system or the mechanism of the marketplace. But we have now gone on so long in a controlled situation, so far as energy is concerned, that the system has been so mained, so distorted, so injured, that there is no way for this patient to walk without crutches. You cannot do what has been done to the energy industry over the past ten to fifteen years and then bless it and say, "You are now on your own in the market system; get up and walk." I believe, therefore, that what Mr. Carter did, supplementing the market pricing system with certain kinds of governmental action, was absolutely essential.

Of course, the market system—the pricing system—will eventually get the large cars off the road, but will it do it in time? I do not think so. The market system will bring shale plants on line at some time, but will it do it in time for the present problem which we face as a nation? I do not believe so. Therefore, I believe that the market system at this time and in this particular situation has to be supplemented by certain kinds of governmental incentives.

I attended the Camp David meetings but I did not write the tablets which President Carter brought down from the mountain; I handed him a chisel. The program that came down from the mountain, now going through the Congress, contains three thrusts in addition to the program for control.

The Government Energy Plan

The first thrust is to provide a mechanism for balancing our environmental needs and our energy needs in time. The second thrust provides some means for getting new energy sources on stream available to the American people, perhaps before they otherwise would have been available. And the final thrust is a whole series of things to encourage conservation in the sense of more efficient use of energy.

We all recognize that the need to balance the environment and energy exists. All of us are schizophrenic; we all want clean air, clean water, and an environment in which we can live; and we all want a growing economy. We have been reconciling them in the United States, but at the expense of time.

Atlantic Richfield Company discovered the oil on the north slope of Alaska in 1968 and the first barrel was delivered where it was needed—in the lower forty-eight states—in 1977. Another oil company found an extraordinary amount of oil off shore at Santa Barbara around 1965, 750 million barrels of oil. That oil is still there; it has not yet been delivered fifteen years later. On the East Coast they have been trying to build a refinery for twenty years; the East Coast uses one-third of all the refined products of the United States and refines less than one-quarter of its needs. Despite sixteen tries, not one refinery has succeeded.

The Carter administration proposed a "fast track" for prompt action. It proposed an Energy Mobilization Board that would set a schedule for specific energy projects. Suppose they allow a year for a given project, and if all state and governmental agency permits were not in by the end of the year, the Energy Mobilization Board would have the power to issue those permits. We hope it would not have the power to override standards or anything legislated by the Congress. It does not, in any way, eliminate due process, because at the end of that year, when the Energy Mobilization Board issued the delinquent permits, the matter could be adjudicated in the courts. But legal action would be expedited quickly, going immediately to an appellate court in Washington.

The second thrust of the administration's program is the development of new sources of energy. We have in the United States extraordinary resources of coal—probably the equivalent of 800 billion barrels of oil locked up in coal. And we have approximately 130 billion barrels of oil locked up in shale. The economics have always been just a little beyond us.

Atlantic Richfield Company tried to build a shale plant in 1974. At the beginning of 1974, after we had operated a semiworks plant and proved out the technology, our plant was originally estimated to cost about $375 million for producing 50,000 barrels a day. By the end of 1974, the plant was estimated to cost $875 million and the economics went below the acceptable rate of return; therefore, we did not build that plant.

We are now ready to build the same shale-oil plant at a cost of $2 billion. We should have gone ahead with it then, I suppose. But we do believe the administration's program for financial safety nets is essential to getting a wide variety of synthetics off the ground. Just because one large company builds one plant does not mean we are going to get off to any reasonable kind of start, industry-wide, in testing various technologies in synthetics. Therefore, we have supported the administration's concern for at least a modest underpinning of financial safety nets for these first plants. They will be very difficult to operate, and something invariably will go wrong.

Windfall Profits Tax

The third thrust of the president's program is a variety of things having to do with conservation or the efficient use of energy. Consider the windfall profits tax: billions of dollars are collected annually by the federal government. You have seen the spectacle in Washington in recent months of the Congress trying to determine how to spend it. Some of the approaches have been, of course, highly justifiable. The proportion or amount that has been set aside to take care of the poorer segments of our society suffering because of the higher prices of energy is entirely essential. Similarly, the marketplace will not take care of the elderly person who cannot pay his heating bill; society must look after that person. And if Congress wants to support these disadvantaged out of the windfall profits tax, that is fine with me.

Some of the windfall profits tax will also be used for essential kinds of research which the marketplace cannot handle. In the United States we are desperately in need of research in nuclear waste disposal. We will not have a nuclear industry of the kind we need until people are satisfied the nuclear waste disposal problem has been solved. And if some of the funds from the windfall profits tax are used for that purpose, that is all right, too.

Also, we are going to have to use a great deal of coal in this interim period before we get to the renewable sources of energy. Yet we do not know the environmental impact of using a large amount of coal. So if a massive research program financed by the windfall profits tax is used to try to find out some of the environmental impacts of the use of massive amounts of coal, that is fine, too.

The tax reduction aspect of windfall profits tax funds I leave to others to consider. But the most effective use of the windfall profits tax would be as incentives for the more efficient use of energy itself. It has been estimated that you have to invest about $35,000 to produce a barrel of oil per day from synthetics. In order to save a barrel of oil per day, you have to invest about $4,000. On any kind of present value economics, I think that it would seem appropriate to try some of these areas in terms of more efficient fuel use.

These are not "long shots"; no big fix, no man-on-the-moon kinds of projects, no big blueprints, just the actions of millions of people in the United States responding to the high price of energy. Appropriate incentives and disincentives from the government could provide us not only with a vast saving in energy over the next twenty years but also support a way of life that all of us might appreciate.

The people of the United States are beginning to recognize our responsibilities not only for a realistic energy program but also toward the peace of the world. We are beginning to recognize our responsibilities for providing resources for future generations, including clean air and clean water. And I think that in the United States we are now beginning to come together to provide a working model of a democracy, so that we can sell democracy throughout the world not by telling people, not by rhetoric, but by example.

About the Contributors

Hussein Abdallah is the First Under Secretary for International Arab and Energy Affairs, Ministry of Petroleum, Republic of Egypt. Dr. Abdallah also serves as Egypt's representative on the executive bureau of OPEC and teaches petroleum economics at Cairo University. Before assuming his present duties he was a professor of petroleum economics at Kuwait University. Dr. Abdallah received the Ph.D. in economics from the University of Wisconsin in 1966. He is the author of several books, including *Petroleum Economics*, a standard text, and *Market Structure of International Oil*.

Yahia Abdul-Rahman is manager of National Oil Company Contracts, Atlantic Richfield Petroleum Products Company. In his current post Dr. Abdul-Rahman negotiates with worldwide oil firms in the Middle East, Africa, Latin America, and Europe for the purchase of hundreds of thousands of barrels of oil daily. A senior planning consultant on conventional energy sources, he has developed strategic options for several oil, gas, and coal corporations. Dr. Abdul-Rahman received the Ph.D. in chemical engineering from the University of Wisconsin.

Thornton F. Bradshaw, former president of Atlantic Richfield Company, is now with RCA. Mr. Bradshaw was elected president of Atlantic Richfield (then Atlantic Refining Company) in 1964, eight years after joining the firm as assistant general manager. He was formerly a professor at Harvard Graduate School of Business Administration and partner in a management consulting firm. He is currently a member of the board of directors of several major corporations as well as the American Petroleum Institute, Aspen Institute for Humanistic Studies, The Conservation Foundation, and other organizations. He was educated at Harvard College and Harvard Graduate School of Business Administration.

Raggaei El Mallakh is director of the International Research Center for Energy and Economic Development, University of Colorado at Boulder. A distinguished professor of economics at the university, Dr. Mallakh is editor of *Journal of Energy and Development* and author of many publications on energy, trade, and investment in the Middle East. A former consultant to the World Bank, he has received grants from The Ford Foundation, Social Science Research Council, and The Rockefeller Foundation. He is serving presently on the U.S. National Committee of the World Petroleum Congress. A former Fullbright Fellow, Dr. Mallakh received the Ph.D. in economics from Rutgers University.

153

Walter J. Mead is professor of economics, University of California at Santa Barbara. Dr. Mead has been engaged in energy research since 1965 when he began publishing articles on the subject. He has testified before Congress on many occasions regarding energy matters and served as senior economist for The Ford Foundation Energy Policy Project, 1972-1973. A former president of the Western Economic Association, he has served as consultant to the Department of the Interior, Federal Trade Commission, Office of Technology Assessment, and Office of Management and Budget. He received the Ph.D. in economics from the University of Oregon.

L. Calvin Moore is vice-president of the Oil, Chemical and Atomic Workers International Union. Mr. Moore became a member of OCAW in 1954 and served in various capacities before he was elected president in 1966. He served as president until 1975, at which time he was appointed international representative of OCAW serving in the Houston, Texas, area. In 1977 Mr. Moore became OCAW's citizenship-legislative director and served in Washington, D.C. Two years later he was elected vice-president. Among his responsibilities are three of the union's departments: legislative, education and research, and human relations. He is a member of all the OCAW's governing bodies.

Laurence I. Moss is chairman of the Environmental Caucus, National Coal Policy Project. A former national president of the Sierra Club, Mr. Moss has served as chairman of the Environmental Advisory Committee of the Federal Energy Administration. He is director and executive-committee member of Resources for the Future, the Environmental Law Institute, and the Gas Research Institute. He served as a White House Fellow, assistant to the secretary of transportation, and executive secretary of the Committee on Public Engineering Policy of the National Academy of Sciences. Mr. Moss received the B.S. in chemical engineering and the M.S. in nuclear engineering from the Massachusetts Institute of Technology.

Francis X. Murray is director of national programs, Center for Strategic and International Studies. Mr. Murray joined the Center for Strategic and International Studies in 1974 and was appointed director of national energy programs two years later. He is also director of the National Coal Policy Project. Mr. Murray has served as chief of the systems analysis branch, Atomic Energy Commission, and as advisor to the Federal Power Commission on natural gas resources and conservation. At Georgetown University he conducts an energy and foreign-policy seminar. He has also written and lectured extensively. Mr. Murray received the B.S. in business administration and economics from LaSalle College and the M.B.A. in economics and statistics from the University of Nebraska.

Edward A. Myers, Jr., is vice-president, Southern California Edison Company. Mr. Myers joined the electric utility in 1964 as a management consultant. He served in various applications-engineering and communications-activities positions for Edison, and his field of responsibility now covers corporate communications, conservation, community services, and revenue requirements. Mr. Myers is a graduate of the University of California at Berkeley and Stanford University Graduate School of Business Administration.

John Naisbitt is senior vice-president of Yankelovich, Skelly & White, Inc., and head of the Naisbitt Group. Mr. Naisbitt publishes *Trend Report*, a YSW publication. He has served as chairman of the board of the Center for Policy Process, Washington, D.C. He also served as special assistant to President Johnson and HEW Secretary John Gardner. Mr. Naisbitt has wide business experience and is the author of several social and military studies, including *The Multiple Option Society*. His weekly syndicated column, "A Changing America: Trends and Forecasts," appears in many major newspapers.

Andrew Safir, former director of the Office of Economic Policy, State of California, is now in private business. Dr. Safir served as assistant secretary for economic policy for the Business and Transportation Agency of the State of California, where he advised the governor, the legislature, and the business community on economic matters. He was also advisor on domestic and international energy issues to the General Accounting Office. Dr. Safir received the Ph.D. in economics and M.A. in economic theory from Tufts University.

Roger W. Sant is director of Carnegie-Mellon's Energy Productivity Center. The Energy Productivity Center was formed 1977 to evaluate the potential for minimizing energy costs. Before coming to the center, Mr. Sant was assistant administrator for Energy Conservation and Environment in the Federal Energy Administration. He was President Ford's senior advisor for energy conservation and participated in developing early national initiatives for increased energy production. Mr. Sant has considerable business experience and has also taught at Stanford University. He received the B.S. at Brigham Young University and the M.B.A. from Harvard Graduate School of Business Administration.

David Sternlight is chief economist, Atlantic Richfield Company. Dr. Sternlight has been deputy director of the Secretary of Commerce's Office of Policy Department, where his activities included economic, energy, trade, and science-and-technology policy analysis and development. Before that he was director of economic planning for Litton Industries. He has also been a consultant to the United Nations and to UNESCO on energy and economic statistics and computer applications. A lecturer and author, he also works with several international policy and analysis study groups. He received the Ph.D. in economics from the London School of Economics.

David A. Stockman is director of the Office of Management and Budget. As representative from Michigan's Fourth District, Mr. Stockman was a leading House spokesman on energy issues. Opposing excessive government regulation, he was concerned, as a member of the Energy and Power Subcommittee, with issues of clean air, oil and natural gas prices, automobile-fuel economy, and synthetic fuels. His work on the Clean Air Act led to an appointment on the National Commission on Air Quality. Mr. Stockman was educated at Michigan State University, Harvard Divinity School, and Harvard University Institute of Politics.

Jude T. Wanniski is president of Polyconomics, Inc. Mr. Wanniski founded Polyconomics in 1978 to advise corporate and financial clients on political, economic, and communications strategies. He was a Fellow of the American Enterprise Institute in Washington, D.C., where he wrote *The Way the World Works: How Economics Fail—and Succeed*, widely praised for its theory of global economy. A writer and associate editor for the *Wall Street Journal*, Mr. Wanniski received the 1976 Milburn Petty Award as petroleum writer of the year. He received the M.S. in journalism at the University of California at Los Angeles.

Eddie N. Williams is president, Joint Center for Political Studies, Washington, D.C. A former columnist for the Chicago *Sun-Times*, Mr. Williams has experience in politics and academic life. At the University of Chicago he served as vice-president for public affairs and director of the Center for Policy Study. In Washington he has served in the State Department as a Foreign Reserve Officer, as staff assistant in the House of Representatives, and as a Congressional Fellow of the American Political Science Association. Mr. Williams is active on a number of boards of directors, including the District of Columbia Municipal Research Bureau. He was educated at the University of Illinois and Atlanta and Howard Universities.

Margaret Bush Wilson is chairman of the National Board of the National Association for the Advancement of Colored People. In addition to practicing law in St. Louis, she is a member of the bar in Illinois and practices before the Supreme Court. She is a member of many boards, committees, and organizations, including American National Red Cross, United Way of America, Mutual Real Estate Investment Trust, Washington University, and Advisory Committee to the Arms Control and Disarmament Agency. She has received numerous civic and professional awards and honorary degrees.

Timothy E. Wirth is a representative in the U.S. Congress from Colorado's Second District. Mr. Wirth has served on a number of important committees and has been responsible for many congressional reforms. He was a key member of the Interstate and Foreign Commerce Committee and the Committee on Science and Technology. From his position on the Energy and Power Subcommittee, he has helped shape the nation's energy policy, and his interest in solar energy has included the Solar Energy Research Institute in Golden, Colorado. A former Ford Foundation Fellow, he received the Ph.D. from Stanford University.

Eric Zausner is vice-president of Booz, Allen & Hamilton, Inc. Mr. Zausner directs his firm's worldwide energy consulting practice. He has extensive experience in energy policy, strategic planning, forecasting, environmental assessment, and government energy programs. Before this he was deputy administrator of the Federal Energy Administration. As deputy assistant secretary for energy at the Interior Department, he organized the first federal energy conservation office as well as energy activities of the Bureau of Mines, Geological Survey, and other departmental programs. Mr. Zausner received the M.B.A. in finance from The Wharton School, University of Pennsylvania.

About the Editors

Meredith S. Crist received the Ph.D. in economics from the University of California at Los Angeles and taught in micro- and macroeconomics at the University of Southern California Graduate School of Business Administration. Her areas of special interest included regulatory economics and industrial organization. Dr. Crist served a number of public and private clients as a consultant in energy and economics. At the time of her death, just before the publication of this book, she was employed by Booz, Allen & Hamilton, Inc.

Arthur B. Laffer is director of the Center for the Study of Private Enterprise. Dr. Laffer is also Charles B. Thornton Professor of Business Economics at the University of Southern California; a member of the Los Angeles Times Board of Economists; and a member of the policy committee and board of directors of the American Council on Capital Formation. He has served as consultant to the secretaries of the treasury and defense and as economist for the Office of Management and Budget. He was also an associate professor of economics at the University of Chicago. Dr. Laffer received the Ph.D. in economics from Stanford University.

IT

Aoii

Boowe ojr

P-IT